Meeting Skills for Leaders

A Practical Guide for More Productive Meetings

Third Edition

Marion E. Haynes

A Crisp Fifty-Minute™ *Series Book*

This Fifty-Minute™ Book is designed to be "read with a pencil." It is an excellent workbook for self-study as well as classroom learning. All material is copyright-protected and cannot be duplicated without permission from the publisher. *Therefore, be sure to order a copy for every training participant through our Web site, www.axzopress.com.*

Meeting Skills for Leaders

A Practical Guide for More Productive Meetings

Third Edition

Marion E. Haynes

CREDITS:

VP, Product Development:	**Adam Wilcox**
Editor:	**Marguerite Langlois**
Production Editor:	**Genevieve McDermott**
Production Artists:	**Nicole Phillips and Betty Hopkins**

Trademarks

Crisp Fifty-Minute Series is a trademark of Axzo Press.

Some of the product names and company names used in this book have been used for identification purposes only and may be trademarks or registered trademarks of their respective manufacturers and sellers.

Disclaimer

We reserve the right to revise this publication and make changes from time to time in its content without notice.

ISBN 10: 1-4188-6489-7
ISBN 10: 1-4188-6489-7
Library of Congress Catalog Card Number 2005930428
Printed in the United States of America
5 09 08

Learning Objectives for

MEETING SKILLS FOR LEADERS

The learning objectives for *Meeting Skills for Leaders* are listed below. They have been developed to guide the user to the core issues covered in this book.

The objectives of this book are to help the user:

1) Prepare and organize meetings that will accomplish the stated goals

2) Select and arrange facilities and equipment best suited to each situation

3) Conduct meetings that are interactive and productive

4) Lead stimulating discussions and handle conflict effectively

5) Evaluate meeting effectiveness and take steps to improve future meetings

Assessing Progress

We have developed a Crisp Series **assessment** that covers the fundamental information presented in this book. A 25-item, multiple-choice and true/false questionnaire allows the reader to evaluate his or her comprehension of the subject matter.

To download the assessment and answer key, go to www.axzopress.com and search on the book title.

Assessments should not be used in any employee-selection process.

About the Author

Marion E. Haynes is one of Crisp's best-selling authors. He has written 35 articles and ten books on management and supervisory practices, as well as retirement and life planning.

Mr. Haynes served for four years on the board of directors of Sheltering Arms, a social service agency for the elderly in Houston, Texas. He also chaired the agency's personnel committee and served on its executive committee.

He was a member of the board of directors of the International Society for Retirement Planning for eight years, serving as president from 1991 to 1993. He has chaired the editorial board for the society's journal and served on its newsletter board.

Mr. Haynes retired from Shell Oil Company in 1991 after a 35-year career in human resource management. At retirement, he was the manager of pensioner relations.

Today he and his wife, Janice, live in Kerrville, Texas, where he pursues his interest in writing, community service, and travel.

Preface

Meetings are a part of everyday life. Besides meetings that we attend during working hours, nearly everyone at one time or another is a member of a professional society, civic association, service club, or religious group. With meetings occurring so frequently, you would expect them to be a source of satisfaction and accomplishment. However, as your experience probably tells you, this often is not the case.

This book is the third edition of *Effective Meeting Skills*, now titled *Meeting Skills for Leaders*. The new title emphasizes the importance of conducting effective meetings as part of your leadership skills, and specifically addresses ways in which you can develop related skills and techniques. You will also find new content on virtual meetings, which are increasingly part of business life.

This book was designed to help you improve the quality of meetings you lead or attend. It begins with the premise that an effective meeting is one that achieves its objectives within a reasonable time. From there, this book discusses how you, as a leader, can make meetings effective, choose the best facilities and equipment, conduct meetings that will produce positive results, lead effective discussions, and improve your leadership of meetings.

Throughout the book you'll find questionnaires, checklists, and exercises that emphasize the material presented. Work through these as you go along. They serve as an excellent means of verifying your understanding.

Effective meetings are within your grasp—simply read, understand, and apply the ideas contained in this book.

Marion E. Haynes

Table of Contents

Part 1: The Effective Meeting   1

Defining an Effective Meeting...3
Information or Decision-Making? 5
To Meet or Not to Meet...7
Face-to-Face, or Virtual?..9
Developing an Agenda...12
Selecting Participants..15
Notifying Participants 18
Choosing a Meeting Time 19
Solutions to Common Meeting Problems 21
Planning the Effective Meeting...22

Part 2: Facilities and Equipment   25

Guidelines for Facilities and Equipment...27
Meeting Room Checklist 33
Guidelines for Visual Aids 34
Guidelines for Projector Screens 36
Projection Methods 37
Arranging Virtual Meetings 40
Teleconferencing...41
Videoconferencing 43
Computer Conferencing...45

Part 3: Conducting Meetings   51

The Meeting Leader's Role..53
The Major Components of a Meeting...55
Structuring Information Meetings..58
Presenting Information Effectively 59
Conducting a Question-and-Answer Session...61
Structuring Decision-Making Meetings...62
Generating Alternatives...63
Choosing Among Alternatives 65
Criteria-Based Decisions...67
Criteria-Based Rating..68
Criteria-Based Ranking...69
Criterion-Based Paired Comparison 70

Part 4: Leading Effective Discussions   73

Stimulating Discussion 75
20 Tips for Generating Discussion...77
Handling Difficult Situations...83
Understanding Conflict..88
Managing Conflict 90

Part 5: Improving Meetings   99

An Improvement Model..101
Evaluating Meetings 102
Meeting Evaluation Forms...105
Providing Feedback..107
A Model for Effective Meetings 111
The Necessary Steps to an Effective Meeting 114
Being a Productive Participant...119

Appendix   121

Additional Worksheets for Meeting Evaluation................................123
Appendix to Part 1 128
Appendix to Part 2 129
Appendix to Part 3 130
Appendix to Part 4 131
Appendix to Part 5 133
Additional Reading 135

P A R T 1

The Effective

Meeting

Defining an Effective Meeting

A meeting can be defined as a gathering of three or more people sharing common objectives, where communication (oral and/or written) is the primary means of achieving those objectives.

A meeting is effective when:

> ➤ It achieves its objectives

> ➤ It takes a minimum amount of time

> ➤ Participants are satisfied in relation to the time and the objectives

Problems with Meetings

Many people who regularly participate in meetings report a majority of the meetings are ineffective. For example, one survey[1] of 635 executives showed that 75% of them were "bothered" by the ineffectiveness of typical meetings they attend.

Write down three things that bother you about meetings you attend.

1. _____

2. _____

3. _____

Compare your reaction to the meetings you attend to the following negative meeting characteristics listed in the executive survey:

Meeting Characteristic	"Bothered a Lot"
Drifting Off Subject	83%
Poor Preparation	77%
Questionable Effectiveness	74%
Lack of Listening	68%
Verbosity of Participants	62%
Length	60%
Lack of Participation	51%

---

[1] Reprinted with permission from the American Society for Training and Development, from *Training and Development*, "Achieving Effective Meetings—Not Easy But Possible," by Bradford D. Smart. © 1974, American Society for Training and Development. All rights reserved.

EVALUATE A MEETING

Consider the typical meeting you attend, whether in business, in a club, or other setting. Compare your meetings to the following characteristics of an effective meeting. Check (√) those statements that apply to meetings you normally conduct or attend:

- ❑ 1. An agenda is prepared prior to the meeting.
- ❑ 2. Meeting participants have an opportunity to contribute to the agenda.
- ❑ 3. The appropriate and necessary people can be counted on to attend each meeting.
- ❑ 4. Those invited receive advance notice of meeting time and place.
- ❑ 5. Meeting facilities are comfortable and adequate for the number of participants.
- ❑ 6. The meeting begins on time.
- ❑ 7. The meeting has a scheduled ending time.
- ❑ 8. The use of time is monitored throughout the meeting.
- ❑ 9. Everyone has an opportunity to present his or her point of view.
- ❑ 10. Participants listen attentively to each other.
- ❑ 11. There are periodic summaries as the meeting progresses.
- ❑ 12. The meeting is periodically evaluated by participants.
- ❑ 13. No one tends to dominate the discussion.
- ❑ 14. Everyone has a voice in decisions made at the meeting.
- ❑ 15. The decision process used is appropriate for the size of the group.
- ❑ 16. When used, audiovisual equipment is in good working condition and does not detract from the meeting.
- ❑ 17. The meeting typically ends with a summary of accomplishments.
- ❑ 18. People can be depended upon to carry out any action agreed to during the meeting.
- ❑ 19. Following the meeting, each participant receives a memorandum of discussion or minutes of the meeting.
- ❑ 20. The meeting leader follows up with participants on action agreed to during the meeting.

Number of Statements Checked _____ × 5 = _____ Meeting Score

A score of 80 or more indicates you attend a high percentage of quality meetings. A score below 60 suggests work is required to improve the quality of meetings you attend.

Information or Decision-Making?

Meetings can be classified into two major categories according to their purpose: information meetings and decision-making meetings. Each category has two subsets.

Information Meetings:

> ➤ Advising/updating

> ➤ Selling

and

Decision-Making Meetings:

> ➤ Goal/policy setting

> ➤ Problem Solving

This classification is helpful because each type of meeting must be conducted differently.

In some cases, a meeting may combine both types. For example, if the meeting is to decide and create new policies, the first part of the meeting might be conducted as an information meeting, reviewing important information the participants need to do the work. The rest of the meeting would be conducted as a decision-making meeting.

Think About It

List three meetings you have attended or have conducted lately. Were they information meetings, decision-making meetings, or a combination of both?

1. _____

2. _____

3. _____

In the chart on the next page, you will see more specific differences between the two types. Use this chart to classify your meetings and then determine the proper way to plan for each type.

Which Type of Meeting Do You Need?

Elements	Information Meeting	Decision-Making Meeting
Number of attendees	Any number	Small size, preferably 12 or fewer
Who should attend	Those who need to know	Those responsible and those who can contribute
Communication process	One way from leader to participants, with opportunities for questions	Interactive discussion among all attending
Meeting room setup	Participants may face front of room, classroom style	Participants facing each other, conference style
Most effective style of leadership	Authoritative	Participative
Emphasis should be	Content	Interaction
Key to success	Planning and preparation of information to be presented	Meeting climate that supports open, free expression

To Meet or Not to Meet

Deciding on the type of meeting you need gives you a specific way to see what you want to accomplish. Before you go further in your planning, it is important to decide if you really need a meeting to accomplish your objectives. All too often holding a meeting is a quick choice, when it should be a carefully considered decision.

What Are the Objectives?

The decision on whether to hold a meeting should start with a statement of objectives. What are the results you expect to achieve through a meeting? Is a meeting the best way to achieve those objectives?

Here are some examples of meeting objectives:

➤ To inform our department of changes in the holiday pay policy

➤ To sell management on our plans to attract a new type of customer

➤ To decide the best way to solve our organization's budget deficit

➤ To update all staff on the progress of a current project

➤ To determine realistic sales goals for each district based on the company's overall sales goals for next year

➤ To determine the critical skills required for successful performance as a first-level supervisor

With objectives clearly stated, you can then determine the best way to achieve them. It may turn out that a meeting is appropriate. Or it may turn out that an e-mail, a memo, a bulletin board posting, or series of phone calls would be a better approach.

Look again at the examples above. Are there some you think can be achieved without a meeting?

Remember that this takes some thought. For example, it may be that you can inform people about a new pay policy without calling a meeting. On the other hand, if you anticipate a number of questions and want to deal with as many as possible in a specific time, a meeting might be useful.

The questionnaire on the next page will give you some guidelines in deciding if you need a meeting.

Do You Really Need a Meeting?

Information Meetings

Consideration: **Yes**   **No**

➤ Is time of the essence?   _____   _____

➤ Is the group geographically dispersed?   _____   _____

➤ Does the size of the group make a meeting feasible, say 10
to 100?   _____   _____

➤ Is it imperative that everyone fully understand the
information?   _____   _____

➤ Is the information being presented needed later as
reference material?   _____   _____

Decision-Making Meetings

Consideration: **Yes**   **No**

➤ Is the knowledge required for any problem solving
dispersed among several people?   _____   _____

➤ Is the commitment of several people required for
successful implementation of the results?   _____   _____

➤ Can the synergy of group interaction contribute to a quality
decision?   _____   _____

➤ Are there likely to be conflicting points of view that need
to be reconciled?   _____   _____

➤ Are there questions of fairness that need to be resolved?   _____   _____

Think About It

List three meetings you have recently attended or conducted. Did you really need a
meeting? Why or why not?

1. _____

2. _____

3. _____

Face-to-Face, or Virtual?

Telephones, video, and computers all provide options for the "virtual meeting," allowing people to meet and share information without being together in the same place. Virtual meetings can save time and money. They can provide a cost-effective way for people to share information, ideas, discussions, and planning.

There are three types of virtual meetings, based on the technology used. Here is an overview.

Teleconference

Teleconferencing, the oldest of the virtual meeting formats, has been around since the days of the party telephone line. When three or more neighbors were visiting on the party line, they were participating in some of the first conference calls.

Today's teleconferencing has come a long way from the old party line. The technology works well for simple information sharing and straightforward decision-making that require no visual presentation. It is not a suitable venue for discussing more complicated matters. Also, teleconferencing is not a desirable way either to begin or to further important relationships. However, given its limitations, it still can accomplish a lot.

Videoconference

Videoconferencing has the advantage of allowing meeting participants to see one another as they talk. Videoconferencing has been around since Bell Labs introduced its videophone in 1964 at the World's Fair in Flushing Meadow, New York. However, it did not catch on until technology advanced in the field of transmitting and receiving digitized data. Since then, demand has increased dramatically.

Too many people tend to compare videoconferencing to what they see and hear when watching television and conclude that since it is not as good as television, it is not worth using. This is flawed logic, as the two have quite different objectives. The problem is misunderstanding the objective, and is sometimes a technology problem as well. With the right equipment, videoconferencing can be very effective in transmitting information, and does help communication by allowing people to see one another.

Computer Conference

The widespread use of the Internet and the World Wide Web has spawned a new form of meeting. With the ability to communicate inexpensively, in real time, people are using computers and the Internet, intranets, and the Web to bring geographically dispersed people together for information sharing, collaboration, and problem solving.

Another feature of the Internet that supports and facilitates meetings is an extranet. This is a private Web site that allows those who have access to share files, documents, and use message boards. While these features cannot take the place of a meeting, they can be used quite effectively to share information in advance of either a traditional or virtual meeting. And through ongoing communication and document sharing, they may actually reduce the need for some meetings.

Will a Virtual Meeting Work for You?

Before setting up a virtual meeting, it is important to decide if that is the best way to accomplish what you need to do. Virtual meetings are not for everyone. They work best where you have a group of people who already know each other. It is also useful to get together for some face-to-face time every now and then, since face-to-face meetings provide a different type of interaction. Here are some of the advantages and disadvantages of virtual meetings:

Advantages

➢ **Virtual meetings usually cost less.** The cost of travel has increased substantially. With the savings from travel offset against equipment costs, virtual meetings can easily be the less costly way to get together.

➢ **Virtual meetings save time.** Besides saving travel time, virtual meetings usually are shorter meetings. There is less social interaction, and meetings tend to be more structured and focused.

➢ **Virtual meetings can be arranged more quickly.** When the need to arrange travel is removed, the lead time required to convene a meeting is reduced dramatically.

➢ **Virtual meetings can reach a wider audience.** Virtual meetings can pass information on to a very large number of people at the same time. Videoconferencing and some forms of computer conferencing are particularly well suited to this type of communication.

Disadvantages

➢ **Virtual meetings may hinder group cohesiveness.** Virtual meetings do not facilitate group development. People can't share anxieties, concerns, plans, and problems in the same way they do at face-to-face gatherings. The process of going to a meeting, and mingling with others, can confirm organizational culture and team spirit in a way that virtual meetings cannot.

➢ **Virtual meetings lessen the impact.** A new product or service can be introduced by way of a virtual meeting. But the excitement and feedback opportunities available when everyone is in the same place at the same time will be missing.

➢ **Virtual meetings eliminate informal exchange.** The informal exchange that takes place at face-to-face meetings often is as useful as the official agenda. People who may hardly ever see each other talk over organizational problems and potentials that could never be discussed during a virtual meeting.

➢ **The medium may dilute the message.** Virtual meetings depend on a variety of technologies, and are limited in the way they present and exchange information. In addition, some people may become so absorbed in the technology that they miss the message being presented. Some people believe that these limitations alter the impact and the value of the information.

Think About It

Now answer these questions:

If you have been to a virtual meeting, do you think it worked well?

_____

Why or why not?

_____

_____

Can you think of a meeting topic in your organization that might make a good topic for a virtual meeting?

_____

_____

Why do you think it would work?

_____

_____

Developing an Agenda

When you have decided to have a meeting, and what type of meeting to have, your next step is to develop an agenda. Every meeting should have an agenda, and participants should get it in advance, if possible. In most cases, participants should have an opportunity to contribute to the agenda prior to the meeting. A combination of e-mail and phone calls is usually effective for developing an agenda with input from at least some of the participants.

An agenda need not be an elaborate document, but it should be specific and should be documented in some visible form—as a handout, on a slide, a board, or a flip chart.

The needs of the participants are an important guide when you prepare a published agenda. What do they need to know to effectively participate in the meeting? The following elements should be included:

➤ Date and time of meeting

➤ Meeting objectives

➤ Items to be discussed (listed in proper sequence)

➤ Meeting adjournment time

➤ Time of scheduled breaks, if any

Example of a Meeting Agenda

- Opening statement: reason for attendance, objective, time commitment

- Problems to be discussed (list, if more than one)

- Generate solutions

- Decide among alternatives

- Develop plan to solve problem(s)

- Assign tasks to carry out plan

- Establish follow-up procedures

- Summarize and adjourn

Other Agenda Considerations

When you are planning or leading a meeting, there are other details you need to consider related to your agenda. Paying attention to these will help ensure that your agenda is an effective tool.

The Leader's Agenda

As leader of a meeting you need more detail than the participants. For example, you should have an approximate time allocation for each item, to properly gauge the progress of the meeting. Also, you may need notes on techniques to use, points to clarify, and equipment that may be required.

Sending the Agenda

When sending an agenda prior to a meeting, think about who should receive a copy. Determine those who should receive a copy strictly for information and those you expect to attend and participate in the meeting. Address your transmittal to those you expect to attend. Show the information-only recipients as cc's. This will clear up any uncertainty that may exist over who is expected to attend.

Sending the agenda ahead of time allows participants to think and prepare for the meeting. You can get your agenda out by e-mail, by posting it in a visible place, or by written memo. It usually works best if each person has a copy. Be sure to have extra copies of the agenda at the meeting, for people who forget to bring their copies.

For Regular Meetings

Regularly scheduled staff or committee meetings seem to be the most common violators of the agenda requirement. One way to overcome this problem is to take five minutes at the beginning of the meeting to develop and post an agenda. If there are several items on the agenda, prioritize them so you can deal with the most important ones in the time available. If new items come up during the meeting, add them to the agenda in proper priority order.

PREPARE AN AGENDA FOR YOUR NEXT MEETING

Think of a meeting you are likely to conduct in the near future. Consider items to be discussed and the sequence in which they should be handled. Estimate the time required for each item. From this estimate, set a tentative ending time. (**Note:** Consider this a tentative agenda until you review it and confirm it with participants.)

Agenda Item	Time Estimate

Selecting Participants

When selecting meeting participants, the best guideline is to have the smallest number of appropriate people. This is not always easy. There often will be people who feel they should come, but they are unable to contribute and will not gain from attendance. Also, there may be people you feel you should invite because of their position in the organization, but they too may have nothing to contribute.

The only feasible method for selecting participants is to consider the type of meeting you are planning.

➤ If it will be an *information meeting*, you want attendees who need to know the information being presented or who will contribute to presenting the information.

➤ If it will be a *problem-solving meeting*, you need participants who have knowledge to contribute, authority over the area affected by the decision, and the commitment to carry out the decision.

Before the meeting, give some thought to those who might wish to attend but are not on your participant list. To maintain good relationships, it may be wise to explain the objective of your meeting to them, and why you feel they do not need to attend. They will probably react by:

➤ Agreeing with you and saying thank you for your thoughtfulness

➤ Disagreeing with you and presenting reasons that may cause you to change your mind

➤ Disagreeing with you but requiring you to stand firm on their exclusion

The information on the following page will give you more details to aid you in selecting participants for your meetings.

Criteria for Information Meeting Attendees

➤ **Need to know the information:** Attendees should be people who will need to use the information, or who will be affected by it.

➤ **Need to get the information at the same time:** Some people may not need the information immediately, and can get it later in some other reliable way. If so, these people do not need to attend the meeting.

➤ **Ability to ask important and useful questions:** The question-and-answer session has a lot to do with the success of an information meeting. People who can contribute to it effectively will help achieve the goal of the meeting.

➤ **Ability to support the implementation of the information:** If there are people who will be key in implementing the information, you may want them to attend the meeting.

Criteria for Problem-Solving Meeting Attendees

➤ **Knowledge of the subject area:** You need people who represent the various aspects of the expertise required to develop a valid solution to the problem.

➤ **Commitment to solving the problem:** Group members should have a vested interest in solving the problem.

➤ **Time to participate:** Each person must have time to participate in problem-solving activities.

➤ **Diversity of viewpoints:** The group must be able to look at a problem in different ways to avoid patterned thinking.

➤ **Expressiveness:** Group members must feel free to express facts, opinions, and feelings.

➤ **Open-mindedness:** When members are willing to listen to each other, and to change their minds when they are convinced by compelling arguments, they can reach the best solution.

WHOM WILL YOU INVITE?

Whom in your organization would you invite to these kinds of meetings?

1. A meeting to discuss a major change in a project plan:

   _____

   _____

   _____

2. A meeting to inform people how to handle the most frequently asked questions about a new company policy:

   _____

   _____

   _____

3. A meeting to determine your department's goals for next year:

   _____

   _____

   _____

4. A meeting to discuss why a project is not going well and to propose solutions:

   _____

   _____

   _____

Notifying Participants

When you invite people to a meeting, you need to send them the information they will need to be able to attend, take part, and deal with their needs for food and other accommodations if necessary.

The following checklist summarizes things most participants need to know in order to attend and participate in a meeting. Use it as a model for your meetings.

For all participants:

❑ Meeting date and time

❑ Meeting place

❑ Directions to meeting place

❑ Meeting agenda

❑ Any advance work they need to do

❑ Any material they need to bring

❑ Proper attire

❑ Parking arrangements if necessary

❑ Meal arrangements if necessary

❑ Whom to contact to request adaptations for disabilities

Additional items for out-of-town participants:

❑ Travel arrangements

❑ Accommodation arrangements

❑ Billing instructions for items such as:

   ❑ Travel

   ❑ Hotel

   ❑ Meals

   ❑ Parking

Choosing a Meeting Time

Certain days of the week and selected times of the day are better than others for holding meetings. Give careful thought to your meeting time so your participants can be present, on time, and ready to engage in the business of the meeting.

Considerations for Your Meeting Time

Include the following when you plan for your meeting time:

> **Preparation time.** How much time will it take you and the participants to do the necessary preparation work?

> **Your availability.** If you are leading the meeting, or need to be a participant, what time will work for you?

> **Facilities.** When will an appropriate and comfortable meeting space, with the facilities and equipment you need, be available?

> **Participant availability.** What options for meeting time do your participants have? Current office software suites often include message programs that make this step much easier.

When choosing a time to meet, avoid late afternoons before a holiday or weekend, or early mornings following a day off. Be willing to be creative. For example, consider meeting during the noon hour with a brown bag lunch, or before the start of the official work day with a continental breakfast.

Meetings of non-business groups such as civic associations or professional societies must meet outside of normal work hours. They face more of a challenge to find an acceptable meeting time. These sessions will typically fall in the evening during the week. If you are part of a small group, explore the possibility of meeting at other times acceptable to all involved, such as various weekend or meal times. Remember, if facilities are available and everyone is willing to meet, any time is acceptable.

Use the worksheet on the following page to tentatively schedule or reschedule some of the meetings for which you are responsible.

PICK A TIME FOR YOUR MEETINGS

Use this worksheet to tentatively schedule or reschedule some of the meetings for which you are responsible. Don't arbitrarily eliminate unconventional times.

	Monday	Tuesday	Wednesday	Thursday	Friday	Saturday	Sunday
6:00							
7:00							
8:00							
9:00							
10:00							
11:00							
12:00							
1:00							
2:00							
3:00							
4:00							
5:00							
6:00							
7:00							
8:00							
9:00							
10:00							
11:00							

This page may be reproduced without further permission.

Solutions to Common Meeting Problems

This list is an overview of specific steps you can take toward more effective meetings. Check (√) those you most want to implement or improve.

❑ **State Your Objective**

Every meeting needs objectives. They should be clearly presented in the leader's opening statement. This simple procedure establishes the reason for the meeting. With an objective in mind, participants can direct their discussion and energy to that goal.

❑ **Prepare an Agenda**

An agenda is essential. You should prepare one and give it to participants in advance. This will serve as a road map to keep discussion on the topic. When distributed before a meeting, an agenda encourages advance preparation.

❑ **Manage Meeting Time**

Strike a balance between wasting time and railroading the group. Allow sufficient time for participants to become involved and feel satisfied with the outcome. Start on time and keep things moving toward an announced ending time.

❑ **Take Charge**

Effective control and guidance are required for effective meetings. Use the agenda to keep the discussion on topic. Encourage less active participants to contribute. Control those who attempt to dominate. Determine ahead of time the best procedures for achieving the meeting's objective and use them at appropriate times.

❑ **Close with a Summary**

Every meeting should close with a restatement of the meeting's objective, a summary of what was accomplished toward the objective, and a review of agreed-upon action that needs to be taken.

Planning the Effective Meeting

As you can see from the previous pages, planning an effective meeting requires attention to detail. The following questions are a practical guide for your planning.

➤ Will the meeting be an information meeting, or a decision-making one?

➤ Do you really need to meet?

➤ Do you need a face-to-face meeting, or will a virtual meeting work for you?

➤ What will be on the agenda?

➤ Who needs to attend?

➤ When and where will you meet?

CHECK WHAT YOU LEARNED

Consider each of the following statements and mark it true or false based on the material in Part 1.

**True or
False**

_____ 1. A meeting relies on communication to achieve its objective.

_____ 2. An effective meeting must consider the satisfaction of all participants.

_____ 3. Effective meetings can consume unlimited time.

_____ 4. A majority of business executives are bothered by the ineffectiveness of the meetings they attend.

_____ 5. Drifting off the subject is a common complaint about meetings.

_____ 6. Information meetings are best conducted in a participative style.

_____ 7. Decision-making meetings can be conducted through interactive group discussions.

_____ 8. Decision-making meetings can be conducted with any number of participants.

_____ 9. It is a good idea to invite everyone who wants to come to any particular meeting.

CONTINUED

**True or
False**

_____ 10. In developing an agenda, you need to consider topics, priorities, and time.

_____ 11. Face-to-face meetings are usually best if you want a lot of open discussion.

_____ 12. Virtual meetings do not allow sharing of documents.

_____ 13. When you choose the time for meetings, one of the first considerations is preparation time.

_____ 14. A virtual meeting is generally less expensive than a traditional meeting.

_____ 15. A virtual meeting can be an effective team-building venue.

_____ 16. A teleconference can be an effective way to hold briefing sessions.

_____ 17. A meeting is always the best way to disseminate information to a large group of people.

_____ 18. A group can normally solve a problem better than an individual.

_____ 19. Typically, staff meetings don't need agendas.

_____ 20. An agenda is an effective means of controlling the discussion in a meeting.

*Compare your answers to the author's recommended responses
in the Appendix.*

PART 2

Facilities and Equipment

Guidelines for Facilities and Equipment

The meeting room, furnishings, and equipment will contribute significantly to an effective meeting. When facilities are effective, they go unnoticed. When they are inadequate or too elaborate, they can detract from the meeting.

Choosing On-Site or Off-Site

On-site meeting rooms are usually convenient and low cost. This makes them attractive considerations. However, being convenient for participants also makes them convenient for interruptions. Occasionally, an on-site room will not be the right size for a particular meeting. Be willing to look elsewhere for a proper meeting place.

Planning for Physical Comfort and Special Needs

Pay attention to the participants' physical comfort. Chairs should be comfortable, especially if the meeting will last over an hour. Heating/cooling, lighting, and ventilation should be adequate for the size of the group and activities planned. You may also need to consider adaptations and space if any people attending have disabilities.

Providing Tables

A table is required only when it has a use (for example, to write on or spread out maps, charts, and computer printouts). While tables are standard in most meeting rooms, consider your need. Perhaps a better room arrangement would be available without a table. However, if you want participants to take notes, or if you know some will be bringing laptops, provide tables for comfortable writing.

Setting Up the Room

When setting up the room, consider the communications needs for the type of meeting you plan to hold. Usually, you want those talking with each other to maintain eye contact. Therefore, information meetings should have participants facing the front of the room, if that will be the best way for them to see the speaker. For a smaller group, you can use a U-shape. Decision-making meetings should have participants facing each other. Examples of different room arrangements are shown on the following pages.

Sample Room Arrangement for Information Meeting

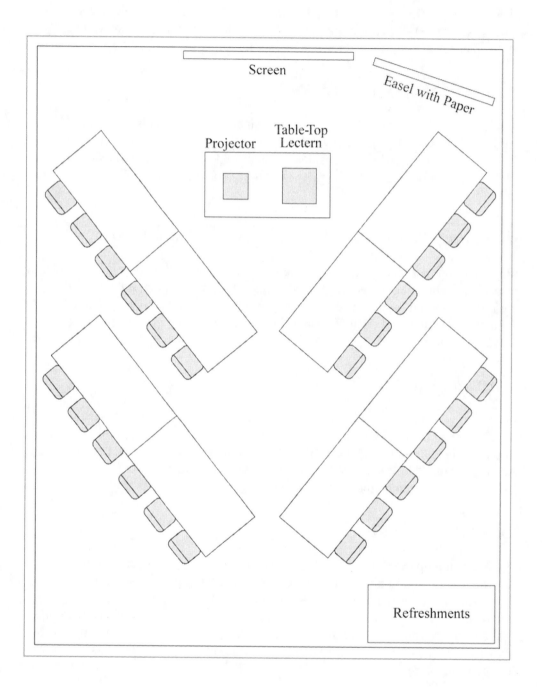

Sample Room Arrangement for Information Meeting

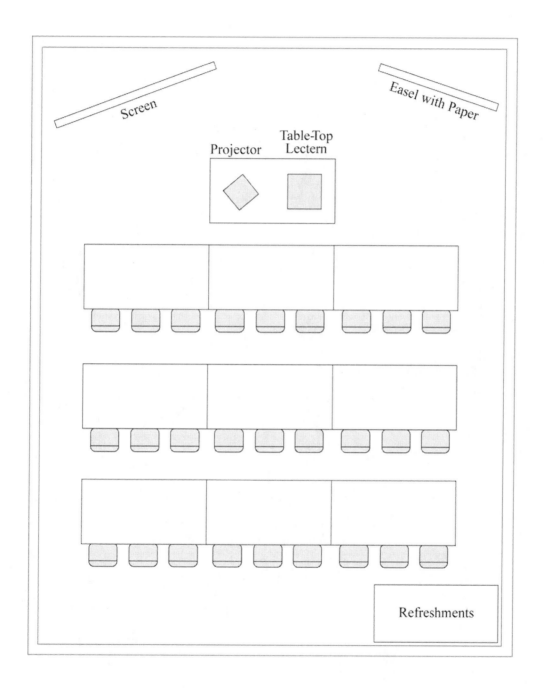

Screen

Easel with Paper

Projector

Table-Top
Lectern

Refreshments

Sample Room Arrangement for Either Type of Meeting

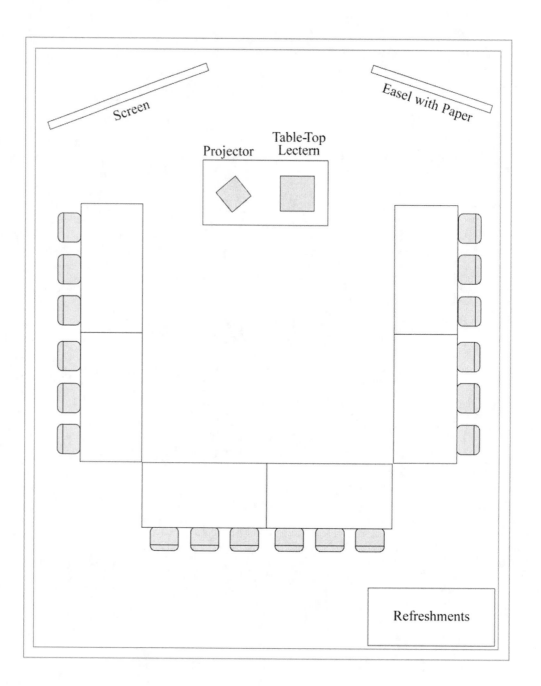

Sample Room Arrangement for Decision-Making Meeting

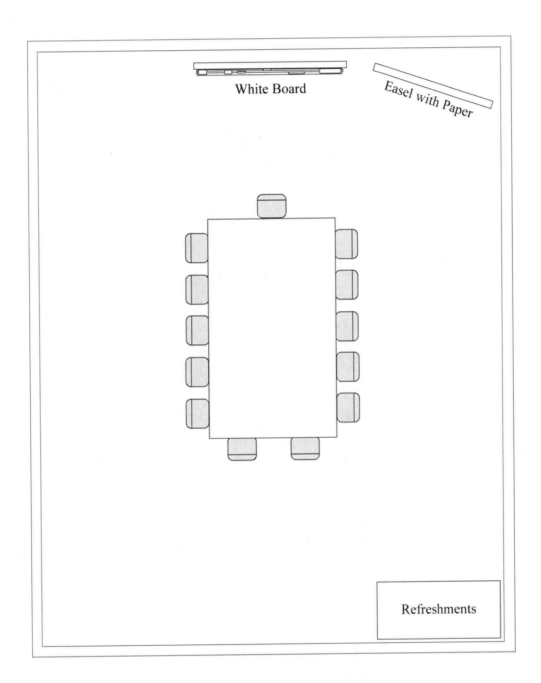

Sample Room Arrangement for Decision-Making Meeting

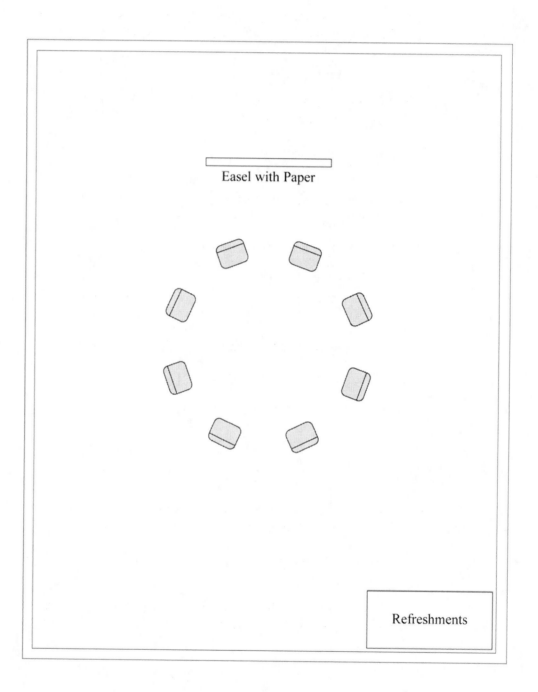

Meeting Room Checklist

The following checklist summarizes the key requirements for an acceptable meeting room. Use it to see if a potential meeting room will meet your needs.

Yes/No

_____ 1. Is the room large enough to comfortably accommodate the participants and any planned audiovisual aids or equipment?

_____ 2. Is there adequate lighting and ventilation? Can they be controlled within the meeting room?

_____ 3. Is the room free from distractions and interruptions, such as telephones, loud noises, or other activities?

_____ 4. Is the room appropriately furnished? Are the chairs comfortable enough for the length of the meeting?

_____ 5. Will the room allow you to make any needed adaptations for participants with disabilities?

_____ 6. Is the room conveniently located for participants?

_____ 7. Is the cost of the room within budget?

_____ 8. Is the room available at the time you need it?

Think About It

Think of a meeting you have attended lately. Did the facilities work well? If so, in what way? If not, what could have been done to make them work more effectively?

_____

_____

Think of a meeting room or conference room that gets a lot of use in your office or organization. What things could you change that would improve the space for any future meetings in that room?

_____

_____

Guidelines for Visual Aids

Well-designed visual aids are helpful in both information and decision-making meetings. Today, the most common type of visual aid is a computerized slide presentation, such as PowerPoint, although flip charts or overhead transparencies are still viable options. Visual aids should help guide the meeting—*not* become the entire focus of the meeting. Use visual aids to:

➤ Stay focused on key points

➤ Simplify complex content

➤ Focus attention on discussion points

➤ Display graphs, data, pictures, drawings, or illustrations

Designing Visual Aids

When creating visual aids:

➤ Use a white, soft blue, or light gray background so information is easy to view

➤ Use large letters and stay away from all capital letters (which is too difficult to read)

➤ Use a simple type style, and only one or two different fonts

➤ No more than two colors that contrast with background

➤ Keep formatting simple:

    ➤ No more than two colors that contrast with the background

    ➤ No more than six lines per visual

    ➤ No more than four to six words per line

If you have more information for the participants than you can put on the individual slides or transparencies, use handouts as well.

Think About It

Think about meetings you have attended lately. Have you seen any visuals that were well presented, and that made their point clearly? What made them work well?

_____

_____

_____

_____

_____

_____

_____

Think of a topic you might present at a meeting. What points would be good to put into visuals? Create some ideas in the boxes below.

Guidelines for Projector Screens

There are a few simple guidelines for the proper placement of screens and projectors, room orientation, and screen size that, when followed, will contribute to an effective meeting.

1. Screens must be placed to allow clear viewing by all in attendance. Care must be exercised so that the speaker and projector do not obstruct the view of the screen.

2. Place the screen to the speaker's right (if right-handed) to allow easy access for changing visuals or writing.

3. Matte finish screens provide a clear image when viewed at angles down to 25 degrees. Beaded and lenticular screens do not perform well at this sharp of an angle.

4. The speaker should be located at one end of a room's narrow dimension.

5. The proper size of a screen is determined by the distance to the person seated furthest from it. See the table below.

6. Screens must be tilted forward at the top (or back at the bottom) to prevent image distortion known as keystoning.

Screen-Size Table					
Distance to Screen	20 ft.	25 ft.	30 ft.	35 ft.	40 ft.
Screen Size	50"×50"	60"×60"	70"×70"	84"×84"	96"×96"

Projection Methods

As more and more people rely on computers—especially laptops—for business and personal use, many businesses provide LCD projectors for use during meetings, and rental and purchase prices have come down as well. Technology has also improved to the point that, often, using the projector is just a matter of "plugging in" your laptop and you're off and running!

How to Ensure a Stress-free Laptop Presentation

➤ **Start with a top quality computer.** If you will be using your own laptop, buy one with as much speed and storage capacity as you can afford. It is frustrating for both you and your audience to wait for the next visual to load.

➤ **Check the computer.** Whether using your own computer or one provided at the meeting site, try your presentation on it before the meeting. If you will be using your own laptop, be sure that it has all the features you need, including a port to connect the LCD projector cable. With a laptop, it's also important to be sure your battery is fully charged.

➤ **Use a remote mouse.** This will free you to stand away from your computer and move about the meeting room.

➤ **Turn off the screen saver.** It is very distracting if it comes on during your presentation.

➤ **Back up your material.** Carry a second presentation on CD, disk, or jump drive.

➤ **Back up your presentation.** In case equipment fails, have an alternative ready, such as a set of transparencies so you can switch to an overhead projector if needed, or be sure there is another computer or laptop available that you can use.

Other Points to Consider

If an LCD projector is not available, you might find out if an overhead projector or even a 35mm slide projector is available. A business services provider could transfer your PowerPoint or word processing file to transparencies or slides. This method can be more costly and time-consuming, however.

Keep in mind that when you are displaying slides or overheads, participants' focus may be on the visual rather than on the speaker. If the visuals become too distracting, you may want to turn off the projector after a slide has been presented so people can focus on the discussion.

If you have a small meeting, and simple information to convey with visuals (no illustrations or complex graphs), you might consider simply using a prepared flip chart.

Whatever projection method you decide to use, be sure to practice using it ahead of time to avoid glitches during the meeting.

EQUIPMENT CHECKLIST

Whatever type of visuals you use, be sure to have the proper equipment and to check it all carefully before you start. Here is a suggested checklist you can use.

- ❑ Screen placed so that all participants can see it easily and clearly

- ❑ Screen placed to the speaker's right or left, depending on the speaker's preference, to allow easy access for changing visuals or writing

- ❑ Screen and the projector arranged to eliminate image distortion as much as possible

- ❑ Screen size that works well with the size of the room

- ❑ Projection equipment conveniently placed for speaker

- ❑ Extra bulbs for slide or overhead projector

- ❑ Extension cords and power strips as needed

- ❑ Tape for taping down cords

- ❑ Laser pointer if needed by speaker

Additional for Computer Presentation

- ❑ Power cords as needed

- ❑ Extra batteries if using laptop

- ❑ Remote mouse

- ❑ LCD projector with power cord and connecting cable

- ❑ Backup CD, disk, or drive

Arranging Virtual Meetings

When arranging a virtual meeting, you need to pay even more attention to facilities and, especially, to the equipment. You have a tightly specified time for your meeting, you are connected to people in other locations and probably other time zones, and any equipment problem will result in lost time, frustration, and perhaps the need to reschedule.

General Guidelines

➤ Select a room away from noise and distractions. When you are listening on the phone or via computer or video broadcast, noise from outside makes it harder to hear participants. The noise may also be carried to the other meeting locations over the equipment.

➤ If several people are participating from a shared location, have ample space for participants to sit comfortably, where they can hear and see well, take notes, and all share equipment as needed.

➤ Get information, documents, and any other needed material to participants well ahead of time, so you do not use valuable meeting time distributing these things.

➤ Check all the equipment ahead of time. If you set it up a day or more ahead, check it again just before the meeting starts.

➤ Because some of the participants will be present only by phone, video, or computer, be sure to set up a meeting protocol in advance that ensures all participants can have their say.

A Word About Terminology

There is a lack of consistency in terms used in everyday language to describe types of virtual meetings. Some writers use *teleconferencing* to mean all forms of virtual meetings. Others use the term *electronic meetings*. Terms like *Web meetings*, *net meetings*, and *e-meetings* are often used in place of computer conferencing.

For the sake of simplicity and consistency this book uses terms related to the technology used: *teleconferencing* when telephones are used, *videoconferencing* when video technology is used. When a computer is the basic tool, whether the communication is written, audio only, or audio and video, the term is *computer conferencing*.

Teleconferencing

Perhaps the easiest form of virtual meeting is a telephone conference. You may already have taken part in this kind of meeting. In many larger organizations, teleconference equipment is already part of telephone equipment, at least in some conference rooms and/or work areas. Many basic phone packages come with the option to bring at least a third person into a conversation. Most telephone companies offer teleconference services and can help you choose and install equipment if it is not available already.

Basic Formats for Teleconferences

The Conference Telephone Call

This type of teleconference works well when the people who need to communicate are located in a variety of locations. The equipment may already be in place in your office, and you may have telephone technical support people who will set up the call for you. If not, your telephone service or long-distance carrier can set up the meeting for you. They will need date, time, and list of names and telephone numbers of conference participants. A telephone company employee will take it from there and get everyone together at the appointed time. Arranging with your long-distance service provider for a conference call telephone number may be a less expensive, and more convenient, method. These numbers can be either toll or toll-free. Participants call the number at the appointed time, enter a participant code, and are connected to the conference.

One-to-Group Teleconferencing

A format often used for teleconferencing is to convene a face-to-face meeting in a room that has been outfitted with teleconferencing equipment. Then, one or two people call in from another location. This format is effective when the input of one person is essential to a group's problem solving or decision-making. It facilitates two-way communication so that everyone in the meeting can fully understand the input of the remotely located person. This format is also effective for information meetings, such as briefing sessions.

Group-to-Group Teleconferencing

The third format ties two face-to-face meetings together. Each meeting room has teleconferencing equipment, including adequate speakers and microphones. Everyone taking part can hear all that is said in both locations, and can speak to both locations. This type of virtual meeting can be effective for sharing ideas between two groups. It can also be used for simple problem solving and decision-making with groups that already know each other.

Dealing with Common Teleconference Problems

➢ **Noise:** Choose a meeting space that cuts out as much outside noise as possible. The acoustics of the meeting environment can be a major problem when holding a teleconference. Background noise will be picked up on microphones and interfere with sound quality. Also, room design can contribute to echoing that produces further interference.

➢ **Leadership:** A virtual meeting conducted via teleconference, like any other meeting, requires leadership to be effective. A major role of the leader, or moderator, is to see that everyone has an opportunity to participate. You may wish to set up the speaking order ahead of time or rotate through participants in a specific pattern. Be sure to call on each person at least once during the meeting. At the end be sure that everyone has a chance to add further comments if needed.

➢ **Speaking Order:** In face-to-face meetings, people can use visual signals to determine who will speak next. There are no such signals in a teleconference. This can be handled in several ways. In the group session of a one-to-group teleconference, and in both sessions of a group-to-group teleconference, a moderator can direct the order of speaking. Conference calls usually have few enough participants that this is not a problem. In addition, it may be helpful if participants who don't know one another identify themselves when they speak.

➢ **Printed Materials:** In a teleconference, you cannot hand out materials as you do in a face-to-face meeting. Remember to send out printed materials in advance to all participants, and be sure they arrive in time. You can use e-mail, fax, or time-priority shipping.

Think About It

Have you ever taken part in a teleconference? Did it work well for you? For the other participants?

_____

_____

Could anything have been done to improve the meeting? If so, what?

_____

_____

Videoconferencing

Videoconferencing requires specialized equipment in all of the places where participants will gather. Larger businesses have sometimes installed the equipment. One or more cameras and television monitors are required at each site along with microphones. Remote-controlled cameras, sound mixers, and control boards can run up the costs. Added to that is the cost of equipment for quality data transmission.

Basics Formats for Videoconferencing

One-to-One

One-to-one meetings, also known as point-to-point, involve full two-way audio and video between two locations. This technology works very well with individuals or groups where the objective is to share information. Either portable or permanently installed equipment can be used. The best quality is obtained from a permanent studio installation.

One-to-Many

One-to-many broadcasting involves full audio and video transmission from a main site that may be a conference room with portable equipment or a studio with permanent equipment. In some cases, remote sites may be able to send only audio. For example, in a teaching situation, the lecturer can see the students while they ask questions, but the students cannot see the lecturer. In addition to its application in education, this format can be quite effective for allowing a high-ranking person to address one or several meetings at the same time.

Many-to-Many

Also known as multi-point communication, this format provides full audio and video communication among more than two sites. With most multi-point systems, participants can see only one site at a time; switching between sites has to be planned and controlled carefully. The many-to-many format requires complex bridging equipment to make sure every location can send and receive signals from every other site.

Dealing with Common Problems

➤ **Cost:** Videoconferencing can be expensive. One way to eliminate the capital investment and depreciation of equipment is to use the services of an off-site company. These companies have state-of-the-art conference room studios in various locations where you can convene groups. Groups are then linked together into a conference. Other types of videoconferencing companies can bring the needed equipment to your locations. Videoconferencing companies are available in most major cities.

➤ **Quality:** High-quality videoconferences require equipment that is capable of transmitting and receiving high-quality signals. This equipment must then be operated by trained technicians. With one-to-many broadcasts, the use of a state-of-the-art studio will generally produce the best results.

➤ **Camera-Shy Participants:** Many people are uncomfortable being "on camera." This feeling is probably heightened in a studio setting as opposed to a conference room. A practice run before the conference convenes can help overcome these feelings.

➤ **Application:** Videoconferencing contributes to meetings where it is either helpful or important that participants see who or what is being shown on camera. Sometimes this feature is more distracting than helpful. Just because a conference room is outfitted for video transmission and reception does not mean it should be used.

Think About It

Have you ever taken part in a videoconference? Did it work well for you? For the other participants?

_____

_____

Could anything have been done to improve the meeting? If so, what?

_____

_____

Computer Conferencing

The combination of Internet access and Web access, now commonly available in most businesses and organizations, provides a number of ways in which people can share information, ideas, documents, and conversation. Internet providers, as well as companies that specialize in Web conferencing or interactive online meeting services, can provide a variety of services related to computer conferencing. Intranets and extranets also facilitate this kind of computer conferencing.

Computer conferencing offers a great deal of flexibility. It can be used for audio, video, file sharing, file editing, and screen sharing. Systems are available for Windows, Macintosh, Linux, and UNIX operating systems.

Basic Formats for Computer Conferencing

Point-to-Point

A point-to-point conference involves two locations. Participants in each location have the needed equipment for both speaking and sharing information visually. This format can include cameras set up so that participants can see each other in addition to the information they are sharing. This format is effective in collaboration and information sharing between people in two locations.

Multicast

A multicast originates with one person and is received by many at various locations. Communications flow back and forth between the originator and recipients, but not between recipients. Using a desktop computer, these conferences can be either audio only, or audio and video. The audio stream can be augmented by visuals on the computer monitor. This format works well for disseminating information and can be used effectively in educational settings.

Multipoint

Multipoint conferences work the same way as point-to-point conferences, but several locations are involved. Each participant must have compatible hardware and software. This format can be used effectively for sharing information, problem solving, and elementary decision-making.

Combined Computer and Phone Conference

Participants can also use software that allows them to share and review documents and other information by computer while they talk to each other using phones set up for a conference call. This format has become relatively simple to set up and is increasingly popular. You may already have software that has the needed options; it is now often included in basic office computer packages.

Dealing with Common Problems

Video Quality: The quality of visual information shared over the Web depends largely on the quality of Internet connections and on the quality of the monitors of the participants. If participants are using cameras, the video quality of those images also depends largely on the equipment.

Audio Quality: If participants are using phones for speaking with each other, the audio quality is usually reasonably good. Audio sent via computer speakers is usually quite good, although it falls short of normal telephone standards. Remember that with long-distance transmission, there may also be a brief time delay. Quality is often better when a conference call provides the audio.

Cost: Internet and intranet connections are now common in most organizations. The software needed for information exchanges via the Web often comes with office suite software. If the participants use telephones for discussion, the cost for that is the same as any telephone conference. There are additional costs for cameras and quality speakers. Think carefully about what you need and examine a range of options before adding equipment.

Firewall: Some firewalls may create computer conferencing problems. If you run into a problem, or think it may be a problem before you start, consult the technical support for your organization or for your firewall software.

Bandwidth: Bandwidth can be an issue. Video is very bandwidth "hungry," and this creates problems for both Internet links and intranets. Some organizations, particularly smaller ones, are finding that when everyone starts using computer conferencing, their present capacity is not sufficient. Telephone and Internet service companies can usually help with this problem.

Confidentiality: Today's office environment poses potential risks to keeping certain information confidential. As with all computer use, virtual meetings can create possible confidentiality problems. The solutions are the same as for any computer security: care in who sees, sends, and receives material; care in who might overhear discussions; and care in use of passwords.

Think About It

Have you ever taken part in a computer conference? Did it work well for you? For the other participants?

_____

_____

Could anything have been done to improve the meeting? If so, what?

_____

_____

CHECKLIST FOR VIRTUAL MEETINGS

When you set up a virtual meeting, pay attention to the same considerations you think of when setting up any kind of meeting, plus a few more, as indicated on this checklist.

- ❏ All equipment arranged for several days ahead of time

- ❏ All equipment in place and checked before the meeting

- ❏ If teleconferencing, either in itself or as part of a computer meeting, all arrangements made for participants to call in as scheduled

- ❏ All needed material and instructions sent to participants ahead of time

- ❏ If participants will meet in a specific room: room comfortably set up with ample space for whatever equipment needed

- ❏ Meeting room away from noise and other distractions

- ❏ If participants will be using computers: computers and software checked ahead of time for compatibility

- ❏ If using videoconferencing: all equipment checked ahead of time

- ❏ If videoconferencing: participants have time to practice ahead of time

- ❏ Extra equipment available in case any equipment fails

- ❏ Technical support available in case problems arise during meeting

---

This page may be reproduced without further permission.

CHECK WHAT YOU LEARNED

Consider each of the following statements and mark it true or false based on the material in Part 2.

True or False

_____ 1. The wishes of participants are important when choosing a meeting time.

_____ 2. Meeting facilities can affect a participant's attitude.

_____ 3. Participants' physical comfort is an important consideration when choosing a meeting place.

_____ 4. Desired communications patterns influence the arrangement of the meeting room.

_____ 5. A classroom-style arrangement is best for a problem-solving meeting.

_____ 6. A conference table is required in every meeting room.

_____ 7. A computer presentation is the most trouble-free type of presentation, since it uses state-of-the-art equipment.

_____ 8. A currently popular and effective format for a virtual meeting is to combine a telephone conference with computer Web networking that allows all participants in all locations to see the same information while discussing.

CONTINUED

Answer the following:

1. When you are preparing visual aids to use in a meeting, what are three of the design elements you can use to be sure your visuals are clear to the audience?

   _____

   _____

   _____

2. When you are having a virtual meeting, what can you do to ensure that all the participants contribute, even if they can't see each other?

   _____

   _____

   _____

Compare your answers to the author's recommended responses in the Appendix.

Conducting

Meetings

52

The Meeting Leader's Role

The meeting leader must focus the energy and attention of participants and keep them moving toward the meeting's objectives. This can be a complex task.

To be an effective leader you must be able to:

➤ Stay focused and keep the group focused

➤ Analyze each situation

➤ Determine what is needed to move forward

➤ Take the necessary action to achieve the objectives

Setting Meeting Ground Rules

Behavior in meetings is based on experience. From their experiences, people make assumptions about what is proper. The way to deal with these assumptions is to set ground rules.

One of the first things you can do to help ensure meeting effectiveness is to establish ground rules specifying how participants are to behave. As meeting leader, you may set these rules yourself, or you may set them through discussion and agreement with participants. If the meeting is a one-time event, the first approach is suggested. If the same participants meet regularly, a participative approach might be better.

With a group that has met for several sessions, ask the question: "What do we typically do in our meetings?" Then classify what is identified as either detracting from, or contributing to, the group's effectiveness. (Some things can be dropped as inconsequential.) Finally, develop ground rules to overcome detracting behavior and reinforce contributing behavior. Ground rules may be set in the content, interaction, and/or structure areas.

Examples of meeting ground rules:

➤ The meeting will begin on time.

➤ Group members will help set the meeting agenda.

➤ Participants will raise their hands rather than jumping in or interrupting someone.

➤ Decisions will be made by consensus.

➤ Conflict is okay.

➤ Expression of feelings and opinions is encouraged.

PRACTICE SETTING MEETING GROUND RULES

Consider a group you meet with regularly. Think of things that typically happen and classify them as either detracting from, or contributing to, group effectiveness. Then, draw up some tentative ground rules around these behaviors.

Detracting Behavior	Contributing Behavior

Ground rules to overcome detracting behavior and reinforce contributing behavior:

1. _____
2. _____
3. _____
4. _____
5. _____
6. _____
7. _____

The Major Components of a Meeting

As a meeting leader, you can understand your multi-faceted role better if you understand the three major components of a meeting.

➤ **Content**

The information, knowledge, experience, opinions, ideas, myths, attitudes, and expectations that participants bring to the meeting.

➤ **Interaction**

The way participants work together while processing the meeting's content. Includes feelings, attitudes, and expectations that bear on cooperation, listening, participation, trust, and openness.

➤ **Structure**

The way in which both information and participants are organized to achieve the meeting's purpose.

An effective leader is attentive to each of the above meeting components. The meeting leader's role is to monitor progress and provide direction. In some meetings participants help provide direction. This makes the leader's job easier. In other meetings the leader is required to provide most of the direction.

The chart on the following page is an outline of activities that may be appropriate for each component of a meeting.

Activities Involved in Conducting Meetings

The leader's role is to monitor the activity in each key component area and provide the missing elements required to move the group toward the meeting's objectives.

Content	Interaction	Structure

➤ Initiate Action
 	
➤ Keep on Topic
 	
➤ Elicit Information
 	
➤ Compare/Contrast Viewpoints
 	
➤ Summarize
 	
➤ Test for Decision
 	
➤ Develop Action Plans
	➤ Monitor Participation
	
	➤ Encourage Participation
	
	➤ Model Supportive Behavior
	
	➤ Encourage Building/ Supporting
	
	➤ Encourage Differing/ Confronting
	
	➤ Facilitation Conflict Resolution
	
	➤ Explore Reactions and Feelings
	
	➤ Facilitate Feedback Among Members
		➤ Develop Agenda
		
		➤ State Objectives
		
		➤ Manage Time
		
		➤ Use Procedures & Techniques for
		  – Recording/ Displaying Data
		  – Analyzing Data
		  – Generating Alternatives
		  – Making Decisions
		
		➤ Make Role Assignments
		
		➤ Develop Ground Rules

MEETING LEADERS YOU HAVE KNOWN

Compare two meetings you have recently attended, one that worked well and one that did not. Think about what you have read in the last two pages. In your two meetings, what were the main differences in how the leaders handled the meeting?

_____

_____

_____

_____

_____

_____

_____

_____

Did you see anything in what you have read about leading a meeting that you could do to improve your leadership of meetings?

_____

_____

_____

_____

_____

_____

_____

_____

Structuring Information Meetings

Information meetings need structure to ensure that participants get the information accurately and completely, and that they have a chance to get their questions answered to ensure understanding of the information presented.

An information meeting works well when it has a structure similar to this:

1. An overview of the meeting's purpose

2. A well-developed agenda and ground rules

3. A well-structured presentation of the information

4. An orderly and informative question-and-answer session

Questions to Ask in Preparing an Information Meeting

➤ What information do participants need about the meeting topic?

➤ How much information do they need to have?

➤ Why do participants need the information—what will they need the information for?

➤ Would it be best to have one meeting for the entire group, or several smaller meetings?

➤ Would it be useful for participants to have some of the information ahead of time?

➤ If so, how and when will they receive the advance information?

➤ Who can best present this information?

➤ Who will conduct the question-and-answer session?

➤ What types of questions do you anticipate?

➤ What will participants do with the information after they leave the meeting?

➤ Will further meetings be needed?

Presenting Information Effectively

Because the primary purpose of an information meeting is to present information, it is critical that you present that information effectively. You want the participants to understand the information, to see how it applies to them and how it affects them, and to leave the meeting feeling that they know what is happening in relation to your topic.

Here is a suggested outline for presenting information effectively:

1. **Opening Remarks**

   The opening remarks should state clearly the topic of the meeting, why this topic is important for those attending, and what the participants can expect from the meeting.

2. **Overview**

   After the opening, present an overview or outline of the material, showing the key points that will be covered in the meeting.

3. **Organization of the Information**

   Organize your information in some logical sequence. Consider using a timeline, or a list of priorities, or starting with the information that will have the most impact. Refer frequently back to the outline, so participants can see where you are going and what has already been covered.

4. **Relation of the Information to the Participants**

   As you go through the presentation, frequently explain clearly what this information means to participants: how it will affect them, and what they will be doing or not doing with the information.

5. **Summary of Main Points**

   As you come to the end of your presentation, review what you have covered in the main points.

6. **Information on Follow-Up**

   Explain to the participants what will happen next, what they can expect, and what is expected of them.

Think About It

Think about the last time you attended a meeting where information was presented.

What worked well about the way the information was presented?

_____

_____

What could have been improved about the way the information was presented?

_____

_____

Conducting a Question-and-Answer Session

The question-and-answer session is an important part of the information meeting. People may want to get more details, or to learn more about how the information will affect them, or to get clarification of certain points.

It is important to build structure and order into these sessions. Otherwise, they can become too long, too short, or chaotic. People can get frustrated about not getting their individual questions answered. Or the behavior of some of the participants may be annoying or even disruptive.

How Do You Conduct a Question-and-Answer Session That Works?

1. **Anticipate questions.** Think ahead about what participants might ask, so you can be prepared to answer. Perhaps building some of the answers into the presentation itself would be effective.

2. **Introduce the person who will answer questions,** if different from the presenter, and explain that person's relevance.

3. **Announce the time allotted for the session.** Tell participants how much time will be devoted to questions and answers. In addition, explain what participants can do to get answers if there is no time for their individual questions.

4. **Lay ground rules.** Explain how you will take questions. Ask participants to raise their hands, and tell them if they need to stand or step to a microphone to ask their questions.

5. **Repeat the question before answering it.** Often, for a variety of reasons, some participants will not hear the question. Repeating the questions also gives the participant a chance to clarify the question if needed.

6. **At the end of the allotted time, thank the participants for taking part.** Explain again how they can get answers for questions not answered, or for further questions they think of later.

Structuring Decision-Making Meetings

Decision-making meetings need structure in order to keep attention focused on the problem. Structure will help maintain the discipline of problem solving. For example, some participants may come to the meeting with solutions to propose. When this happens, work will be required to concentrate on the process of problem solving. The best way to do this to use a technique known as a rational-decision process.

A rational-decision process includes these steps:

1. Study/discuss/analyze the situation

2. Define the problem

3. Set an objective

4. State imperatives and desirables

5. Generate alternatives

6. Establish evaluation criteria

7. Evaluate alternatives

8. Choose among alternatives

When using this process, you first need to spend time discussing the situation and defining the problem. This ensures you are dealing with the right problem. Then, state an objective—the end result you want to accomplish.

If imperatives exist, list them along with the desirable features of your eventual outcome; in other words, list both your needs and wants. If there are mutually exclusive imperatives, each must be reconciled or you cannot solve the problem. Obviously, you want as few imperatives as possible.

Next, generate alternatives, through whatever method you choose. Then, set up some evaluation criteria, evaluate the alternatives against those criteria, and make a decision. You will have come to your decision with a straightforward, orderly process.

Generating Alternatives

You can generate alternatives in several ways. The most common is by open discussion. Two procedures will likely produce more alternatives and reflect greater creativity. These procedures are *brainstorming*, and the *nominal group technique*.

Brainstorming is a free-form process that taps into the creative potential of a group through association. Power of association is a two-way current. When a group member voices an idea, this invites other ideas by stimulating the associative power of all other members.

Nominal group technique has group members write individual ideas, and then report them to the group. It minimizes conformity while maximizing participation.

When choosing between these techniques, consider whether participants have enough experience to deal with the information you seek. If they know the information, the nominal group technique gives you an orderly method for getting it reported to the group. If they do not know the information, brainstorming will create potential alternatives.

On the next page, you can see the procedures for each process.

Remember

When you are generating alternatives, you want ideas to flow freely.
Do not allow evaluations and judgments during this time.

Brainstorming Procedures

➤ List all ideas offered by group members.

➤ Do not evaluate or judge ideas at this time.

➤ Do not discuss ideas except perhaps briefly to clarify understanding.

➤ Welcome "blue sky" ideas. It is always easier to eliminate than to accumulate.

➤ Allow repetition. Do not waste time sorting out duplication.

➤ Encourage quantity. The more ideas, the greater the likelihood of a useful one.

➤ Avoid being eager to close out this phase. When a plateau is reached, let things rest and then start again.

Nominal Group Technique Procedures

➤ Each member writes out ideas in response to the question presented to the group.

➤ Group members take turns reporting what they have written, one idea at a time. List the ideas in front of the group.

➤ Members add new ideas to the list after the group has finished reporting.

➤ The group continues the process until all ideas are listed.

Think About It

At the last decision-making meeting you attended, how did the group gather ideas and generate alternatives?

_____

_____

Could the process have been improved? How?

_____

_____

Choosing Among Alternatives

After group members have produced a number of alternatives, they need to decide which alternatives they will choose to study further or implement. Several decision-making procedures are available to groups during meetings. These tend to be either individual-centered or group-centered. Individual-centered procedures are consolidations of individual choices, while group-centered procedures rely on discussion and agreement.

The decision-making methods most commonly used in meetings are voting, consensus, and the nominal group technique. Let's look at each of these in more detail.

Voting

This form of decision-making is appropriate in larger groups. It should be used in small groups only as a backup style, or when the decision being made is not critical. You can decide based on simple majority, or, to reduce resistance to the final decision, you can set a higher number of votes needed to make the decision, such as 60% of the votes.

Consensus

This form of decision-making maximizes the support of the decision by participants. By nature, it is a highly interactive process and tends to produce quality decisions with a high level of commitment.

The consensus process makes full use of available resources and resolves conflicts creatively.

Consensus is sometimes difficult to reach, so not every group decision can be made in this way. Consensus is not the same as complete unanimity. However, each individual should be able to accept the group's decision on the basis of logic and feasibility. When all group members feel this way, you have reached a consensus, and can state the group's decision. Following are some guidelines to achieve consensus:

> ➤ **Avoid arguing for your position.** Present your position as lucidly and logically as possible, but listen to the other members' reactions and consider them carefully.

> ➤ **Do not assume that someone must win and someone must lose** when discussions reach a stalemate. Instead, look for the next-most acceptable alternative for all parties.

> **Do not change your mind simply to avoid conflict.** When agreement seems to come too quickly and easily, think further. Explore the reasons for the agreement and be sure everyone accepts the solution for basically similar or complementary reasons. Yield only to positions that have objective and logically sound foundations.

> **Avoid conflict-reducing techniques** such as voting, averaging, and bargaining. When a dissenting member finally agrees, do not feel that person must be rewarded by being allowed to "win" on some later point.

> **Differences of opinion are natural and expected.** Seek them out and try to involve everyone in the decision process. Disagreements can help the group's decision; with a wide range of information and opinions, there is a greater chance that the group will hit upon a more adequate solution.

Nominal Group Technique

This form of decision-making minimizes conformity and moves participants to decisions that they can support. As in the nominal group procedure for generating ideas, this process starts with the participants putting their choices in writing. The steps involved are:

1. After discussing the alternatives, individual members independently rate each alternative on a numerical scale, against an agreed upon criterion, such as time or cost.

2. Members report their ratings for each alternative, and the ratings are then added together.

3. If a clear choice appears, the process is complete. If not, alternatives with low total ratings are dropped from the list.

4. Members again discuss and rate the remaining alternatives independently. Again, if no clear choice appears, the alternatives with the lowest ratings are dropped from the list.

5. This process is repeated as required until a clear group choice remains.

Criteria-Based Decisions

Whatever decision process the group uses, setting criteria for choices is an important step. These should be concepts that are important in the implementation of the ideas. You may already have them chosen before the meeting starts. For example, project completion time may be a priority, or the solution must work for several different departments. Sometimes, these concerns come up as part of the discussion. Or the group leader may ask members to set these criteria just before the group begins the decision process.

Think About It

Think about a meeting you attended recently where decisions were made. What were the criteria used or discussed for evaluating alternatives?

_____

_____

Were these criteria useful and important in this situation? Why, or why not?

_____

_____

The charts on the following pages provide examples of using criteria in decision-making processes.

Criteria-Based Rating

After agreeing upon appropriate criteria such as feasibility, availability, and affordability, the group rates each alternative on either a numerical scale or a low, moderate, high scale. You can accomplish this by discussion or by consolidating individual ratings. Here is an example.

Sample Criterion-Based Rating Worksheet

List appropriate criteria across the top. (Usually one to four will be sufficient.) The final choice will be the alternative that rates the best on the most criteria. In this example, the group has used high, moderate, or low rankings.

Alternatives	Criteria		
	1. Time	2. Cost	3. Possible Start Date
1. *Buy new software*	Low	High	Low (soon)
2. *Create new software*	High	Moderate	High
3. *Change procedures*	Moderate	Unknown	High
4.			
5.			
6.			
7.			
8.			
9.			
10.			

Note: Evaluations can be either on a subjective scale such as High, Moderate, Low; an objective scale such as 1 to 5 or 1 to 10; or actual values can be used, such as price, weight, or delivery time.

This form may be copied without further permission.

Criteria-Based Ranking

In criteria-based ranking, the members rank each alternative for a single criterion. After all the alternatives are ranked, members base their final choice on the alternative that ranks highest overall, or go on to further discussion and ranking. Here is an example.

Sample Criterion-Based Ranking Worksheet

List participants' individual rankings (for participants A, B, C, and so forth) and then add across to get a total of individual rankings. In this example, since there are only three alternatives, the one considered best will be ranked 1. For example, participant A feels that buying new software is the best alternative, so has ranked it 1.

Criterion: Cost

Alternatives	Participants' Rankings							
	A.	B.	C.	D.	E.	F.	Total	Group Ranking
1. *Buy new software*	1	1	2	3	2	1	10	1
2. *Create new software*	2	2	3	1	1	3	12	2
3. *Change procedures*	3	3	1	2	3	2	14	3
4.								
5								
6								
7.								
8.								
9.								
10.								

Criterion-Based Paired Comparison

List each alternative twice—on a horizontal line and the corresponding vertical line. Compare alternative 1 to alternative 2. If 1 rates higher put an "X" in the box; if 2 rates higher leave blank. Continue across comparing 1 to all the other alternatives then go to the next line and repeat the process until all pairs have been compared. Count the "X's" across for each alternative and enter the number in the far right column then transfer the totals to the line at the bottom of the chart labeled "number of "X's". Count the blanks down and enter in the appropriate line at the bottom. Add the number of "X's" and Blanks for each alternative and enter in the line marked "Total". The largest total will be the number 1 choice, next highest number 2, etc. In case of a tie, go back and compare the two again.

Yes = X
No = Blank

Alternatives										
	1.	2.	3.	4.	5.	6.	7.	8.	9.	10.
1.										
2.										
3.										
4.										
5.										
6.										
7.										
8.										
9.										
10.										
Number of Blanks										
Number of X's:										
TOTAL										
Priority										

Number of X's

From: *Management by Objectives and Results for Business and Industry,* by George L. Morrisey (Addison-Wesley Publishing Co. 1977). Used by permission of the author.

CHECK WHAT YOU LEARNED

Respond to each of the following questions based on material presented in Part 3.

1. What are two of the benefits of ground rules in meetings?

   _____

   _____

2. The three major components of a meeting are:

   a. _____

   b. _____

   c. _____

3. When you are structuring an information meeting, you need to:

   a. _____

   b. _____

4. Question-and-answer sessions should always be part of an information meeting.

   ❑ True   ❑ False

CONTINUED

5. The reason for following a structured decision process is:

☐   a. To use the synergy of group interaction

☐   b. To make it easier to run the meeting

☐   c. To give everyone an equal opportunity to participate

6. Two techniques for generating alternatives were presented: brainstorming and nominal group technique. Under what conditions would you choose one over the other?

_____

_____

_____

_____

_____

7. Voting is the best form of decision-making in small meetings.

☐ True   ☐ False

8. Consensus decisions tend to be the highest quality decisions made by group.

☐ True   ☐ False

9. Rankings and ratings are based on criteria agreed on by the meeting group.

☐ True   ☐ False

Compare your answers to the author's recommended responses in the Appendix.

Leading Effective

Discussions

Stimulating Discussion

Whether meeting participants are generating alternatives, considering pros and cons, or making choices, the success of any discussion depends on participation. When participants see that a mutual sharing of opinions and ideas is welcome, there is an atmosphere of free exchange. The leader's skillful use of questions will encourage productive discussion.

As a leader, you need to pay close attention to what is happening in the group. Notice if some members seem to be inactive. Pay attention to the pace of discussion. Watch for cues from the group that suggest problems. If participants begin to fidget, look bored, or show by their expressions that they do not understand or that they disagree, you should ask questions to find out what is going on and keep discussion flowing.

There are four types of questions that are helpful in stimulating discussion:

> **General questions,** which elicit a broad range of potential responses.

> **Specific questions,** which focus on a single idea, leaving a limited range of responses.

> **Overhead questions,** which you ask the whole group, allowing volunteers to respond.

> **Direct questions,** which you ask a selected individual.

General and *overhead* questions are less threatening and therefore are better to start a discussion. *Direct* and *specific* questions are best used after participants become comfortable with group discussion.

Things to Avoid

> **Unanswerable Questions**

Be sure that the questions you ask can be answered by the group or by some member of the group.

> **Questions of Simple Assent or Dissent**

Unless followed by other questions like why, when, where, how, what, or who, a yes or no answer leads nowhere.

> **Vague, Indefinite, Ambiguous Questions**

To get satisfactory answers, you must ask good questions. Sometimes you may need to rephrase your question or break it down into sub-questions if it is not immediately understood. Above all, never try to play with words or trap a participant into an incorrect or misleading answer.

> **Forceful Words**

You may have to ask a participant questions in the interest of clarification, but remember that you are not out to prove anything. Your approach should never be one where the person answering feels threatened.

20 Tips for Generating Discussion

The following examples of questions and statements provide some useful guidelines for generating discussion.

#1 Ask for Feelings and Opinions

Ask questions that will help people express their ideas, draw people out, and encourage discussion. For example:

➤ What is your reaction to...?

➤ How do you feel about...?

➤ What is your thinking on...?

➤ What brings you to conclude that...?

➤ What are some other ways to get at...?

#2 Paraphrase

One way to help people reach mutual understanding is to paraphrase, that is, to repeat what someone else said and state what that person meant:

➤ Are you asking me to...?

➤ Let me see if I understand your position. Are you saying that...?

➤ Before we go on, let me paraphrase what I think you are proposing.

➤ Let me restate your last point to see if I understand.

➤ Before you go on, do you mean that...?

#3 Encourage Participation

Sometimes people tend to hold back. You can encourage them to participate with such questions as:

➤ Lee, what do you think about this?

➤ Austin, how would you answer Sherri's questions?

➤ Before we go on, I'd like to hear from Brook on this.

➤ We have heard from everyone but Jane. Jane, what do you think?

➤ We haven't heard from Jack yet. Jack, how do you feel about this?

➤ Let's give Tony a chance to tell it the way he sees it.

➤ Dave, you had your say. Now it's Harold's turn. Give him a chance to explain.

#4 Ask for a Summary

When there is a lot going on in a meeting, sometimes it is helpful to pause and summarize before people go further, with questions like:

- ➤ A lot of good ideas have been presented in the last few minutes. Will someone please summarize the major points before we go on?

- ➤ I have heard a number of proposals. Will someone summarize what has been agreed upon?

- ➤ It is clear Jim does not agree. Jim, will you summarize your major objections?

- ➤ We seem to be off track. Will someone summarize what has been done so far?

#5 Ask for Clarification

When something does not seem clear, ask questions to clarify meaning:

- ➤ I didn't understand that last comment. What did you mean you would do if...?

- ➤ The examples you gave concern weekday operations. Do they also apply to weekends?

- ➤ I saw Maureen shaking her head. Maureen, would it help if we took a minute to explain how these new instructions apply to your department?

- ➤ It is still not clear to me. What did you say we usually do when...?

#6 Ask for Examples

Examples can provide clarification and help the group move along:

- ➤ Dana, will you give some examples of what you mean?

- ➤ Jose, can you expand on that? I'm not sure I understand.

#7 Initiate Action

Asking for action, or for suggestions for action, can help a meeting move on productively:

- ➤ How do you think we should...?

- ➤ Frank, how would you suggest that we proceed on this?

- ➤ I'd like some suggestions on possible ways to get started. Pierre, how would you propose we get started?

#8 Explore an Idea in More Detail

This is a good way to get further information on the topic or ideas being discussed.

➤ What are some other ways to approach this problem?

➤ Are there other things we should consider?

➤ Robin, what would you add to what has been said?

#9 Do a Quick Survey

You can find out where the group is with simple questions:

➤ Let's see a show of hands. How many are for this proposal?

➤ Kira, why don't you ask the others what they think about your proposal?

➤ How does everybody feel about this? Let's start with Luis.

#10 Suggest a Break

When a group shows signs of being tired, or has been working for a long time, a break is useful:

➤ We have been working on this problem for quite a while. How about a quick stand-and-stretch break?

➤ We have been working for about and hour and a half. How about a 10-minute break?

#11 Suggest a Procedure

You can provide guidance for the group with questions such as:

➤ I noticed that Carla has done most of the talking on this issue. I suggest we go around the table to see what others think.

➤ Would it help if we put the agenda items in order of importance before we started?

➤ Let's go around the table so that everyone gets a chance to comment on this.

➤ Let's stop the discussion for a few minutes. I think it might help if we each told the group what we're feeling right now.

#12 Share Your Feelings

Letting the group know how you feel can help them move along:

➤ I feel you are not giving Kerry a chance to explain his position.

➤ I'm frustrated. I think we should take up this problem next week when we have more facts. What do the rest of you think?

#13 Reflect What You Think Someone Is Feeling

This is another way of checking on what is happening with individuals:

➤ George, I get the impression that you are not satisfied with my answer. Is that right?

➤ Kim's comments tell me that he needs to ask some questions on this—is that right, Kim?

#14 Question Assumptions

➤ Your proposal assumes that unless we talk to their managers, they won't cooperate. Is that right?

➤ Your suggestion assumes that we cannot meet the schedule. Is that right?

➤ Your objection assumes that we will not get promised deliveries. Can you explain that further?

#15 Check Targets or Orientation

Questions like these can help you keep the group on target:

➤ Are we asking the right question?

➤ Are these the most important goals?

➤ Is this the best way to get their cooperation?

➤ Is this the only way to get it done?

#16 Confront Differences

➤ Nick, you haven't said so, but I'm sensing that you don't agree. Is that right?

➤ Casey, you seem to be holding back on this. Is there something here you disagree with?

➤ Bridget, I'm not sure you understood what Willie was trying to say. Why don't you tell us what you heard him say before you state your objections?

#17 Role Reversal

➤ Why don't you take the role of a customer for a few minutes. Now, as a customer, how would you react to this proposal?

➤ Pretend you are the district manager for a moment. How would you react to this proposal?

➤ How would you feel if these suggestions were made for our own department?

#18 Look into the Future

➤ If we did it this way, what is the worst thing that could happen?

➤ If it doesn't work, what will we have lost?

➤ If it works, how will it affect next week's schedule?

#19 Test for Consensus

If you think the group is ready to move to consensus, you can check with questions like these:

➤ It seems that we have come to agreement on this issue. Can I have a show of hands on this?

➤ Does everyone accept the idea that...?

➤ Glenda, is that your opinion too?

➤ Before we go on to the next issue, let me check to make sure that all have agreed to...

#20 Focus on Action Choice

➤ We have now considered every possibility. We must choose from these three alternatives.

➤ We have discussed both sides carefully. It's time to make a choice.

EFFECTIVE USE OF QUESTIONS

Select a response from the right column that correctly describes what you would do in the situations described in the left column. Write the letter corresponding to your choice in the blank in front of the number of the situation. (It is okay to repeat a response.)

Situation	Response
____ 1. You want to stimulate discussion.	a. Ask each participant to summarize the other's position.
____ 2. You want to cut off discussion.	b. Ask for feedback from the group.
____ 3. You want to bring a participant into the discussion.	c. Ask the group a general question.
____ 4. Two participants are engaging in a side conversation.	d. Ask one of the individuals a specific question.
____ 5. You are asked a question you are not sure you can answer.	e. Ask the group a specific question.
____ 6. You want to test the level of support for a point of view.	f. Ask the individual a general question.
____ 7. Two participants are debating a point. Everyone else is watching.	g. Ask the group for a summary.
____ 8. Discussion has been going on for some time. You are unclear about progress.	h. Ask an individual to summarize the discussion.
____ 9. Two people have been debating a point without much progress.	i. Direct the question back to the group.
____ 10. You would like to know if you have been an effective leader.	j. None of the above

Compare your answers to the author's recommended responses in the Appendix.

Handling Difficult Situations

Because meetings depend on interaction, it is inevitable that problem situations will occur. Sometimes problems originate with people, sometimes with procedures or logic. In any case, it is the responsibility of the leader to activate discussion of the most profitable kind, to make sure participation is distributed among members of the group, and to keep the discussion headed in the right direction.

Problems with People

It is important to keep good, balanced participation going in any meeting. General participation, with different points of view, is essential for the success of your meeting. Here are some approaches you can use in handling various types of participation problems.

A Person Who Tends to Dominate the Discussion

A talkative participant must not be permitted to dominate the discussion. Sometimes a person may assume a dominant role because of being more experienced or more senior than others present. Often, if that is the case, others will sit back and give up the floor. When this happens, use direct questions to draw out other participants. It is helpful to avoid looking at the senior person when presenting a question, thus making it difficult for that person to get your attention.

If nothing else is effective, a private chat with the individual during a break may help.

A Person Who Wants to Argue

This individual may act like a "know-it-all" or a quibbler who takes delight in crossing up the leader. Usually, such a person irritates the group, inviting unfavorable reactions. In any case, you as leader must remain calm. You can try clarifying questions, which push this person to think about what he or she is saying. Then use direct questions to other participants as a means of maintaining the balance.

Often an argumentative person will recognize what has happened and not present further problems. However, if the person is insensitive, you may have to be very direct, pointing out that the quibbling is interrupting the progress of the meeting and is a waste of valuable time. You should then immediately turn to another person with a question to take the discussion forward.

A Person Who Starts Another Meeting with Neighbors

This problem is more likely to occur in a larger group. It may be the result of a talkative individual's need to speak when unable to address the group as a whole, or it may be the result of a more cautious thinker's desire to try out an idea before bringing it up to the entire group. Side conversations are inevitable in a typical meeting and are apt to be brief. They become a problem only if prolonged.

One technique is to invite the individual to share with everyone what is being said. Another way to handle this situation is to simply be quiet and look at the offending person. Typically, this will bring the meeting back to order.

A Person Who Is Timid or Lacking in Self-Confidence

Whether such a person feels uncertain because of inexperience or is simply unwilling to speak due to fear of embarrassment, you should ask a question in an area where the reluctant individual can speak with conviction. Usually, once the ice has been broken and anxiety dissolved, the individual will become a thoughtful contributor.

A Person Who Is Antagonistic or Skeptical

Sometimes people are antagonistic to the meeting or the leader, or are skeptical about the use of time. Usually such attitudes come from previous experiences with meetings or unskilled leaders. Give these people time. Once your meeting is under way and working well, they may see the difference and begin to participate.

A Person Who Attempts to Get an Opinion Instead of Give One

Experience has taught some people that not all managers or meeting leaders are open to new ideas and tend to force their own views on the group. In this case, participants may reply to questions with another question. In this situation, the best technique is to refer the question back to the group and then back to the one who asked it.

Problems with Procedures

The following situations are impersonal. They call for a different kind of response.

Establishing and Holding the Interest of the Group

It is essential to activate the group's attention in the opening statement and then motivate them to respond. Use visual aids as the discussion progresses. Case studies for group analysis are also effective. If response lags, change the approach. Keep things moving.

Voice can be an effective tool to help regain interest. If interest is waning, speak more loudly, more rapidly, and with more feeling. Typically this will pick up the energy of the meeting.

Handling Touchy Subjects

Anticipate what touchy subjects may arise and face them squarely. If they are not truly pertinent to the subject under discussion, point that out, referring to the objectives of the meeting. If they are pertinent, remain neutral, insisting on an objective consideration of the question. Do not promise to get action from management, but only to report the conclusions or findings.

Developing Discussion and Avoiding Superficiality

Be prepared to cite specific cases and facts for consideration, if they are not forthcoming from group members. Call on individuals known to have specific relevant experiences, past or present. Encourage members to take issue with trends and to avoid the "bandwagon." Encourage original thought. Probe opinions for factual or conceptual causes. Do not permit oversimplification of anything.

HOW WOULD YOU HANDLE THESE SITUATIONS?

Rank your choices for each of the following situations. For each situation, place a 1 near the answer you favor the most, 2 near your next choice, and then follow with a 3 and a 4.

1. Some participants are not contributing to the meeting although they appear to be attentive.

    _____ a. Monitor the situation to see if it continues.

    _____ b. Ask a noncontributing participant for an opinion or reaction.

    _____ c. Ask the noncontributing participants why they are not involved.

    _____ d. Do nothing. They'll speak up if they want to.

2. You want discussion on a topic but no one is talking.

    _____ a. Ask a general question of the group.

    _____ b. Ask a specific question of an individual.

    _____ c. Ask for feedback on why no one is talking.

    _____ d. Adjourn the meeting due to lack of interest.

3. You notice, through nonverbal cues, that the interest level of the group is fading.

    _____ a. Shorten your agenda and adjourn the meeting.

    _____ b. Take a five-minute break.

    _____ c. Speak more loudly and in a more animated fashion.

    _____ d. Try to start a discussion.

4. You get a question you cannot answer.

    _____ a. Redirect the question to the group.

    _____ b. Ignore the question.

    _____ c. Ask the person who asked the question the reason for it.

    _____ d. Admit you do not know the answer and move on.

CONTINUED

5. A participant is using too much time talking about an item that is not on the posted agenda.

_____ a. Interrupt and point out the need to get back to the agenda.

_____ b. Do nothing and hope the meeting makes some progress.

_____ c. Ask participants if they want to discuss the subject.

_____ d. Tell the participant the topic will be taken up at the end of the meeting if there is enough time.

6. The group is getting away from the objective of the meeting.

_____ a. Let things go as long as everyone seems interested.

_____ b. Interrupt and bring the group back to the agenda.

_____ c. Interrupt and vote on whether to continue this discussion.

_____ d. Take a break so participants can continue the discussion on their own time and reconvene when it is over.

7. Two people, sitting together, keep whispering to each other. It has been going on for some time. You find it distracting.

_____ a. Ask them to share their discussion with the group.

_____ b. Ask them a content-related question to see if they've been listening.

_____ c. Stop talking and look at them.

_____ d. Ignore it and hope they finish soon.

*Compare your answers to the author's recommended responses
in the Appendix.*

Understanding Conflict

Interpersonal conflict in meetings is not necessarily bad. In fact, it can be healthy when handled properly. Therefore, the question is not how to eliminate conflict, but how to capitalize on its constructive aspects. In many instances interpersonal differences, competition, rivalry, and other forms of conflict contribute to the effectiveness of the meeting.

A moderate level of conflict may have these constructive consequences:

➤ Increased motivation and energy to do a task

➤ Increased innovative thinking, through a greater diversity of viewpoints

➤ Increased understanding of a position on an issue, by forcing the advocate of that position to articulate it and support it with facts

➤ Increased understanding of opposing positions on an issue, by forcing participants to listen and then to integrate diverse positions to achieve consensus

When all participants are doing their best, conflict is natural. What is best for one department, for example, won't necessarily be the best for others. Conflict management is a primary skill for conducting effective meetings.

What Causes Conflict?

Conflict occurs when the desires of two individuals or groups appear incompatible. It often occurs when individuals come to a meeting with preconceived ideas about the outcome, rather than planning to work together to find a solution that is acceptable to the group. Here are four classic conditions that often lead to conflict:

➢ **Miscommunication:** People often don't listen well. As a result, misunderstandings occur that may lead to conflict.

➢ **Different Perceptions:** Two or more people experience a common event but come away with different views of what happened.

➢ **Different Values:** Different value systems lead people to define acceptable actions differently.

➢ **Different Preferred Outcomes:** Two or more people want different solutions to the same problem.

CONFLICTS YOU HAVE EXPERIENCED

Note a conflict you have seen in meetings, related to each of the four classic conflict situations. In each case, was the conflict resolved effectively? If so, how?

Miscommunication

_____

_____

_____

_____

Different Perceptions

_____

_____

_____

_____

Different Values

_____

_____

_____

_____

Different Preferred Outcomes

_____

_____

_____

_____

Managing Conflict

How conflict is handled will have a dramatic impact on the group and its members' ability to work together.

There are two dynamics to be sensitive to:

➤ The concern people have for winning a point

➤ The concern for maintaining relationships

Five Approaches

How these two dynamics interrelate determines which of five different approaches to use for dealing with conflict: demanding, problem solving, bargaining, giving in, and delaying. Each is appropriate under the right circumstances. Frequently, however, people do not analyze conflict, and so do not choose an appropriate approach. The tendency is to use a comfortable strategy in all situations. This often leads to addressing conflict improperly, and possibly also damaging important relationships.

As you study these five approaches to conflict and their application to meetings, think of how they might affect meetings you attend or lead.

Demanding

This approach suggests that winning is more important than the relationship. Demanding is aggressiveness that often evokes an aggressive response. While it maximizes the individual's outcome, it is usually at the expense of the relationship because, in demanding, there is a winner and a loser. Most people do not like to lose. When they do, they are often motivated to get even. When conducting meetings, you should work to avoid issues polarizing group members to this extent.

Problem Solving

This approach shows high concern for both winning and maintaining the relationship. It is characterized by both parties working together actively to find a mutually satisfactory solution to a common problem. In a meeting, it requires joint problem solving, which in turn leads to creative solutions with commitment to carry them out.

Bargaining

Bargaining is a retreat or backup position when a solution cannot be reached by demanding or problem solving. It remains moderately high on both concerns, winning and maintaining the relationship. It is most effective when both parties are willing to give a little to resolve their differences. In a meeting, you can help group members use bargaining constructively.

Giving In

With this response, maintaining the relationship is viewed as more important than winning the point. It is also an appropriate response when new information invalidates a position. In meetings you conduct, you may need to help participants find face-saving ways to give up their positions on issues under discussion.

Delaying

Every conflict need not be resolved immediately. Delaying confrontation can be appropriate when the issue is trivial. You can also use delaying temporarily to allow people time to cool off, or to gather additional facts.

Model for Resolving Differences

This diagram illustrates ways to resolve differences, based on the five approaches discussed on the previous page. As you can see, in many cases it is possible to find an approach that avoids a win-lose solution.

Model for Resolving Differences

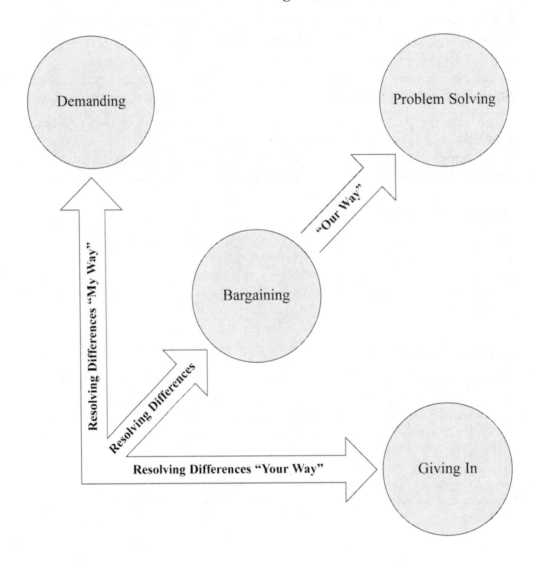

Tips for Moving Through Conflict

When you are leading a meeting, there are specific things you can do to help the group move through conflict. The following ideas should help you handle this in a positive way.

Clarify Objectives

Conflict sometimes develops because participants have different understandings of the meeting's objectives. Clarifying and reaching agreement on objectives is an important first step.

Strive for Understanding

Often, when involved in argument, people do not listen carefully to the opposition's presentation.[1] They are too busy formulating a rebuttal to listen. As the meeting leader, you may find it necessary to stop the action and make sure each party in a conflict can state the opposing party's position and supporting reasons.

Focus on the Rational

Emotional involvement is a natural part of confrontation. However, sound decisions cannot be reached when participants are too emotional. Therefore, for the benefit of the outcome, you should keep attention focused on rational considerations, such as facts, supporting reasons, potential problems if a certain course of action is followed.

Generate Alternatives

What alternate solutions integrate the needs of the diverse points of view involved in the confrontation? This is a challenging part of the process. Participants often cannot see how any alternative to their solution exists. This is where group members not at either extreme can become a resource to generate some reasonable alternatives.

---

[1] For more information on listening, read *The Business of Listening*, by Diana Bonet, a Crisp series book.

Table the Issue

Tabling can be an effective way to deal with conflict when you feel a party needs time to consider the arguments that have been presented. It works particularly well as a face-saving device. People sometimes find themselves in a position of having argued so strongly for a position they cannot gracefully change even after being convinced of the logic of a different position. Tabling gives a person time to work this out.

Use Humor

If you are good with humor you can use it to reduce the emotional tenseness of confrontation. It can serve as a release and clear the way for more rational problem solving.

Other Ways to Handle Conflict in Meetings

Other approaches that can help handle conflict in meetings include:

- ➤ Acknowledging deadlines
- ➤ Involving everyone in the process
- ➤ Allowing time to think
- ➤ Taking a break (i.e., calling a time-out)
- ➤ Referring items to a subcommittee
- ➤ Allowing for expression of strong feelings
- ➤ Protecting the group from early closure

Handling Conflict Between Two Groups

When there is a disagreement between two groups on how to resolve a problem, you can stop the discussion and deal with the conflict in the following way. Ask each group member to indicate where he or she stands on the following scale:

For 5 4 3 2 1 0 1 2 3 4 5 **Against**

When group members have indicated their positions, ask them to post their scores on a flip chart. Then, ask group members who are *for* a given position to explain why other members are *against* the position. Do the same with the other group. Ask those who are against the position to explain why the others are for the position.

In this way, you can:

> ➤ Provide a quick way to get the issues surfaced

> ➤ Get all pro and con ideas out in the open

> ➤ Ensure that each group is listening and understands what the other group is saying and why

Finally, involve those who are neutral on the issue to offer alternatives which integrate the needs of those for and those against.

Conflict should not be avoided in meetings. It is a natural outcome of strongly held points of view. However, it is important to contain it and focused toward resolution.

All conflict can be resolved. Not that it always will—but it can. Most often it is resolved through communication. One expert estimates that 70 percent of conflict can be handled by simply using clear communication. Twenty percent will require negotiation. And the remaining 10% can be resolved through arbitration or the use of a third party.

CHECK WHAT YOU LEARNED

1. When you are leading a meeting, you might use:

    a. Overhead questions to _____

    b. Direct questions to _____

2. Discussion can be generated by:

    ❏   a. Asking general questions of the group

    ❏   b. Asking general questions of individuals

    ❏   c. Providing an authentic opportunity for participants to comment or ask questions

    ❏   d. All of the above

3. All disruptive behavior should be dealt with in the meeting.

    ❏ True   ❏ False

4. Your voice can be an effective tool to help regain interest.

    ❏ True   ❏ False

5. Conflict is to be expected in decision-making meetings.

    ❏ True   ❏ False

CONTINUED

6. Conflict usually results from:

    ❑ a. Lack of communication

    ❑ b. Petty differences

    ❑ c. Different perceptions

    ❑ d. Different preferred outcomes

7. All conflict can be resolved.

    ❑ True   ❑ False

8. All conflict will be resolved.

    ❑ True   ❑ False

9. Which approach to conflict:

    a. Suggests that winning is the most important objective?

    _____

    b. Suggests that maintaining the relationship is the most important objective?

    _____

    c. Usually leads to a mutually satisfactory solution?

    _____

*Compare your answers to the author's recommended responses
in the Appendix.*

P A R T 5

Improving

Meetings

An Improvement Model

Practice makes perfect only when you practice the right things. This section will give you several tools you can use to improve the quality of meetings you attend, whether as a leader or a participant.

The most important element in bringing about improvement is the motivation to improve. As a leader, you may have received feedback that your meetings lacked "something." Or you may have noticed that your meetings tend to drag on and accomplish little. As a participant, you may feel that you want to do more to contribute effectively to meetings you attend. Regardless of what brings you to realize that improvement is in order, nothing will change until you are motivated to make things happen.

The first step will be to single out the elements that need to be changed. This is where input from others is essential. The next few pages go into detail on how to have meetings evaluated. Once improvement areas have been identified, you need feedback on how best to handle those areas.

Finally, when you have developed a new set of actions, it is important to try them. Following each trial, evaluate the meeting to see if the change has been effective. If so, go to the next area that needs improvement. If not, try something else until you solve the problem.

Improvement Model

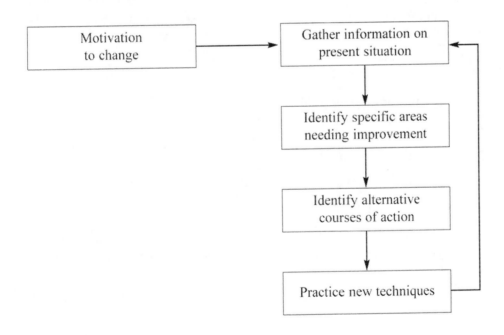

Evaluating Meetings

Effective meetings occur when leaders and participants work to find a better way to get the job done. Participants come to a meeting with ideas, skills, knowledge, and experience. The leader's job is to create an environment where evaluation becomes a normal part of the process.

The benefits of an evaluation will be worthwhile if the following conditions exist:

➤ The leader wants to improve future meetings

➤ The leader receives honest input from evaluators

➤ Evaluators are candid in their assessment

➤ The leader receives feedback in a positive way

➤ The leader incorporates improvements into future meetings

Sources of Evaluation

There are three potential sources for evaluating meetings:

➤ Self-evaluation by the leader

➤ Evaluation by a trained observer

➤ Evaluation by participants

All should contribute to improving a meeting. However, evaluations by trained observers and participants tend to be broader in scope and more objective.

Self-Evaluation by the Leader

After leading a meeting, you should ask yourself:

➤ "How did I do?"

➤ "Where did things go well, and why?"

➤ "Where did I have problems, and why?"

➤ "What would I do differently next time?"

This is the minimum evaluation to be considered. A leader will have impressions about things that went well and problem areas that were encountered. A few minutes reflecting on these experiences can be helpful.

Evaluation by a Trained Observer

A trained observer should be familiar with the ingredients of an effective meeting, skilled in making objective evaluations, and accomplished at giving feedback. It is difficult to find someone with all these qualifications.

A meeting observer typically sits in the back of the room and records notes on an evaluation form. Notes that follow a timeline of the meeting are most helpful. Following the meeting, the observer may either report to the group and invite discussion about how to improve the effectiveness of future meetings. Or the trained observer may choose to report privately to the meeting leader to discuss improvement needs.

Evaluation by Participants

Participants are an excellent resource for evaluation. They have feelings and reactions to meetings, events, and leadership styles that others may not choose to acknowledge. An open discussion is usually useful to get feedback from participants.

Timing of Evaluations

Evaluation can take place during the meeting, at the end of the meeting, or after the meeting has adjourned. Let's look at how you might use each of these.

During the Meeting

This evaluation need not be formal or complicated. During any meeting, the leader can be alert for cues that indicate something needs improving. The cues can be verbal or nonverbal; subtle or blunt. The simplest (and most effective) way is to stop the meeting and deal directly with what is happening.

Another way to initiate an ongoing evaluation is to take time after a break and simply ask the group for comment:

> ➤ "How is the meeting going so far?"

> ➤ "What can we do to make our meeting more effective?"

Give participants time to think about the questions, then ask them to share their comments. Be prepared to listen carefully and respond to suggestions that are made.

At the End of the Meeting

If you have time at the end of the meeting, it might be worthwhile to ask everyone to complete a form and then post the scores on a flip chart for group discussion. The actual numbers are not of special importance. What is important is the opportunity to share perceptions of what is going on. The goal is to deal with items that can improve future meetings.

Use caution with end-of-meeting evaluations. Participants are often in a hurry so they do not take the time to do a quality evaluation. Be sure everyone has enough time to invest in the evaluation or defer it until later.

After the Meeting

If you don't have time at the end of the meeting, or you want to give participants more time to evaluate the meeting, you can use these evaluation techniques:

➤ Distribute evaluation forms to participants as you adjourn asking them to complete and return them to you.

➤ Send evaluation forms to participants soon after the meeting; e-mail is often useful for this.

➤ Telephone a sampling of the group and request a narrative evaluation of the meeting.

➤ Visit with members of the meeting and ask them to evaluate it in a face-to-face discussion.

You will probably get better results if you set a deadline for the return of evaluations.

Meeting Evaluation Forms

The example on the next page illustrates the kind of form that you can use to encourage people to examine their meetings. You will find additional examples in the Appendix. You may wish to select one of these or develop your own.

When you use any evaluation form for a meeting, it is useful to keep it to one side of one page. Participants usually do not want to spend time, either at the end of a meeting or after the meeting, filling out more extensive forms.

No further permission to copy these forms is needed.

MEETING EVALUATION WORKSHEET #1

1. Were the meeting's objectives clearly stated?

   Not At All   1   2   3   4   5   6   7   8   9   Completely

2. Did the meeting meet its stated objectives?

   Not At All   1   2   3   4   5   6   7   8   9   Completely

3. Did the meeting achieve your personal objectives?

   Not At All   1   2   3   4   5   6   7   8   9   Completely

4. Was the knowledge of participants used?

   Not At All   1   2   3   4   5   6   7   8   9   Completely

5. Was decision-making shared by participants?

   Not At All   1   2   3   4   5   6   7   8   9   Completely

6. Did people trust and level with each other?

   Not At All   1   2   3   4   5   6   7   8   9   Completely

7. Were all participants actively involved in the meeting?

   Not At All   1   2   3   4   5   6   7   8   9   Completely

8. Did leadership style contribute to meeting effectiveness?

   Not At All   1   2   3   4   5   6   7   8   9   Completely

9. Which portions of the meeting were most helpful to you?

   A. _____

   B. _____

   C. _____

10. Which aspects were least helpful to you?

   A. _____

   B. _____

   C. _____

11. What action steps will you be taking as a result of this meeting?

   _____

   _____

12. Other comments?

   _____

   _____

Providing Feedback

Feedback allows people to receive information about their effect on others. It can help an individual keep his or her behavior on target and better achieve goals. Consider the following illustration.

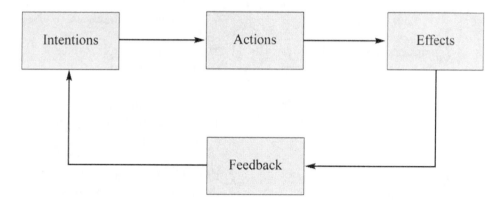

As the leader, it is appropriate for you to provide feedback. Feedback will usually be about an individual's behavior that either helped the meeting accomplish its purpose or was disruptive. It is important to provide positive feedback to participants when they do something that contributes to the meeting's effectiveness.

It is also important for you to be able to receive feedback as a help in improving your meeting skills, whether as leader or participant. When you receive feedback, you can help both yourself and the person giving the feedback by asking questions that produce helpful, specific information.

Criteria for Useful Feedback

➤ **Be descriptive rather than evaluative.** By describing action, you leave the individual free to use or not use the information. By avoiding evaluative language, you reduce the prospect of an individual reacting defensively.

➤ **Be specific rather than general.** To describe someone as "dominating" is not very useful. Instead, you can say something like, "I think you may be missing some valuable ideas in what others are saying" is more specific and helpful.

➤ **Direct feedback toward behavior that the receiver can do something about.** Frustration is only increased when you remind people of shortcomings over which they have no control.

➤ **Time it well.** In general, feedback is most useful at the earliest opportunity after the behavior.

➤ **Communicate feedback clearly.** One way of ensuring this is to have the receiver rephrase the feedback to see if it corresponds to what you had in mind.

Examples of Feedback

Providing helpful, effective feedback is a skill that you can learn. The following examples should give you an understanding of the differences between good and poor feedback.

Poor Feedback	Better Feedback
1. You are crude and disgusting.	1. Your suggestive stories make me uncomfortable.
2. You are rude and inconsiderate.	2. You did not allow me to finish. This makes me feel you don't value my comments.
3. You're unfriendly.	3. I feel like I'm being left out. Is there some reason for this?
4. You're a loudmouth.	4. Because you talked more than others at the meeting, I didn't get a chance to explain my position.
5. You enjoy putting people down.	5. I feel you didn't seriously listen to my point of view.
6. You don't care about anyone but yourself.	6. You seem unconcerned about me and what I can contribute.
7. You ran the meeting all wrong.	7. I'm frustrated that we were unable to come to a decision. What can we do better next time?
8. You are a wonderful person.	8. I am grateful that you came to my defense.

CHECK WHAT YOU HAVE LEARNED
ABOUT EVALUATION AND FEEDBACK

Consider the following statements and mark each true or false.

True or False

_____ 1. Motivation to change is not required in order to improve meetings.

_____ 2. Evaluations can be obtained while a meeting is in progress.

_____ 3. Self-evaluations are usually sufficient to improve meetings.

_____ 4. Trained, unbiased observers can be the most effective evaluators.

_____ 5. Evaluation forms are mainly to record participant reactions in order to stimulate problem solving.

_____ 6. Evaluation forms distributed as you adjourn the meeting generally receive more participant attention than those used as part of the end of the meeting.

_____ 7. More than one attempt at improvement may be required before a problem in conducting meetings is cleared up.

_____ 8. Regularly scheduled staff and committee meetings do not need to be evaluated.

_____ 9. Useful feedback is evaluative rather than descriptive.

_____ 10. Giving helpful, effective feedback is a skill that can be learned.

Compare your answers to the author's recommended responses in the Appendix.

RATE YOURSELF AS A MEETING LEADER

Check (√) yes or no to each of the following questions based on how you act (or would act) as a meeting leader.

Yes   No

☐ ☐   1. Do I have clear objectives for the meeting?

☐ ☐   2. Am I selective about the invited participants?

☐ ☐   3. Do I prepare an agenda and distribute it in advance of the meeting?

☐ ☐   4. Do I arrive early enough to check the arrangements?

☐ ☐   5. Do I start the meeting promptly regardless of who is present?

☐ ☐   6. Do I follow the agenda?

☐ ☐   7. Do I manage time and conclude the meeting as scheduled?

☐ ☐   8. Do I elicit everyone's participation?

☐ ☐   9. Do I help in the resolution of conflict?

☐ ☐   10. Do I maintain proper control of the discussion?

☐ ☐   11. Do I summarize accomplishments at the end of the meeting and clarify any action to be taken?

☐ ☐   12. Do I prepare and distribute a memorandum of discussion?

☐ ☐   13. Do I request evaluative feedback from participants?

☐ ☐   14. Do I take agreed upon action?

☐ ☐   15. Do I follow up on action to be taken by others?

Which two or three behaviors from this list would you like to develop and practice more when you lead meetings?

_____

_____

_____

A Model for Effective Meetings

You can conduct more effective meetings by practicing the ideas presented in this book. This model for effective meetings reviews the most important points you've learned, putting them all together. See also the "Worksheet for Planning an Effective Meeting" in the Appendix.

Meeting Preparation

First, determine whether a meeting needs to be held. Avoid the trap of meeting too often. Be willing to cancel a meeting or adjourn early if there is nothing important to discuss. Deciding whether or not to meet depends on the objective you want to achieve. Once you establish an objective, you may find there is a better way to accomplish it than a meeting.

If a meeting is appropriate, decisions must be made about when and where to meet and who should attend. When choosing a time, keep the needs of participants in mind. Avoid particularly busy times. The meeting site should be comfortable and free of distractions. It should comfortably accommodate the attendees. When choosing participants, be guided by who can either gain from attending or contribute by attending. Keep the number down to the minimum necessary to accomplish your purpose.

Next, develop an agenda and notify participants of the meeting. The agenda should list, in sequential order, items to be dealt with. It also should show the time the meeting begins plus any scheduled breaks and a targeted ending time. A copy of the agenda should be sent to all participants in advance whenever possible. When this is not possible an agenda should be developed as the first item of business.

During the Meeting

The day of the meeting, the leader should arrive at the meeting room early. During this time, it is important to check the room arrangement and change it if necessary. Also, check audiovisual equipment to ensure that it is operational.

Begin the meeting promptly at the scheduled time. An opening statement should include the meeting's objective, a brief review of the agenda, and any appropriate ground rules.

In an information meeting, present information in a clear, concise, easily understood style.[1] Monitor the level of interest as reflected through nonverbal cues. Use voice levels to keep the energy level high. Change the format if interest seems to lag by asking questions. Get the group involved.

In a decision-making meeting, it is essential to facilitate the group's problem-solving and decision-making process. Monitor group interaction and suggest procedures to help make decisions. When there is too little interaction, generate discussion. When there is too much interaction, keep things focused and summarize progress. Techniques for displaying and analyzing data, generating alternatives, and choosing among alternatives will help keep the group moving toward the objective.

Regardless of the type of meeting, close with a restatement of the objective, a summary of what was accomplished, and a list of agreed-upon action that needs to be taken.

After the Meeting

After the meeting, follow up on action points. A brief memorandum of conclusions should be written and distributed. Inform appropriate people who did not attend the meeting about essential decisions made.

Finally, each meeting should be viewed as a learning experience. Future meeting: should be improved by soliciting evaluations and deciding what action steps are required to conduct better meetings.

Good luck! May all of your meetings be productive!

---

[1] An excellent book on this subject is *Presentation Skills*, by Steve Mandel, a Crisp Series book.

The Essential Elements of an Effective Meeting

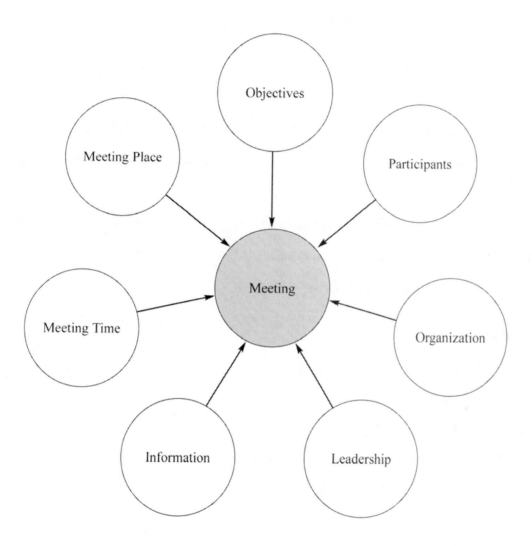

The Necessary Steps to an Effective Meeting

Before the Meeting

Leader:

- ❑ Define objectives
- ❑ Select participants
- ❑ Make preliminary contact with participants to confirm availability
- ❑ Schedule meeting room and arrange for equipment and refreshments
- ❑ Prepare agenda
- ❑ Invite participants and distribute agenda
- ❑ Touch base with non-participants
- ❑ Make final check of meeting room

Participants:

- ❑ Block time on schedule
- ❑ Confirm attendance
- ❑ Define your role
- ❑ Determine leader's needs from you
- ❑ Suggest other participants
- ❑ Know the objective
- ❑ Know when and where to meet
- ❑ Do any required homework

During the Meeting

Leader:

- ❑ Start promptly
- ❑ Follow the agenda
- ❑ Clarify the purpose of the meeting
- ❑ Manage the use of time
- ❑ Limit/control the discussion
- ❑ Elicit participation
- ❑ Help resolve conflicts
- ❑ Clarify action to be taken
- ❑ Summarize results

Participants:

- ❑ Listen and participate
- ❑ Be open-minded/receptive
- ❑ Stay on the agenda and subject
- ❑ Limit or avoid side conversations and distractions
- ❑ Ask questions to assure understanding
- ❑ Take notes on your action items

After the Meeting

Leader:

- ❏ Restore room and return equipment
- ❏ Evaluate effectiveness as meeting leader
- ❏ Send out meeting evaluations
- ❏ Distribute memorandum of discussion
- ❏ Take any action you agreed to
- ❏ Follow up on action items

Participants:

- ❏ Evaluate meeting
- ❏ Review memorandum of discussion
- ❏ Brief others as appropriate
- ❏ Take any action agreed to
- ❏ Follow up on action items

TEST YOUR KNOWLEDGE OF EFFECTIVE MEETINGS

Consider each of the following statements and indicate whether you agree (A) or disagree (D) with it.

Agree/Disagree

_____ 1. A meeting is always the best way to communicate information to a group.

_____ 2. A meeting should be held whenever there is a problem to solve.

_____ 3. A meeting can always be considered effective if you achieve your desired objective.

_____ 4. Most ineffective meetings can be avoided through good planning and preparation.

_____ 5. Effective meetings require the active involvement of all participants.

_____ 6. An important part of preparing for a meeting is to ensure that the right people attend.

_____ 7. Meeting facilities are not important if participants are interested in the subject of the meeting.

_____ 8. Poor scheduling can doom a meeting to failure.

_____ 9. An effective leader should be able to answer all questions asked by participants.

_____ 10. Fear of embarrassment is often the reason for lack of participation.

_____ 11. An effective leader should monitor participation and invite comments from less involved participants.

_____ 12. Questions should be phrased to elicit elaboration on a point.

_____ 13. A good opening statement will help clarify the meeting's objective.

_____ 14. Meetings should start and end on time.

_____ 15. A good summary will include a restatement of the meeting's objective, a listing of accomplishments, and specific action that needs to be taken.

CONTINUED

_____ 16. Participants should leave a meeting feeling that their time was well spent.

_____ 17. Practicing proper techniques helps produce effective meetings.

_____ 18. The leader always knows how well a meeting went.

_____ 19. Proper meeting evaluation includes input from participants.

_____ 20. A trained observer can contribute to improving a meeting's effectiveness.

_____ 21. Participants can do little to prevent a meeting from becoming ineffective.

_____ 22. Others resent a participant who tactfully contributes to an effective meeting.

_____ 23. A summary should be written and distributed following a meeting.

_____ 24. If action items are agreed upon, a confirming memorandum should be sent after the meeting.

_____ 25. Follow-up is often the difference between running a good meeting and achieving results.

Compare your answers with the author's recommended responses in the Appendix.

Being a Productive Participant

We have been focusing on leading meetings, but you can do a lot to make a meeting effective by how you participate in any meeting you attend. Everyone is a meeting participant at one time or another. An effective meeting depends on productive participants. As a participant, you are in a position to make a significant contribution to the success of meetings you attend. All you need is a tactful way to ask questions and offer suggestions.

A productive participant demonstrates all the behaviors previously mentioned for successful meetings. This includes being on time, not carrying on side conversations, being willing to ask questions, paying attention, listening, and staying involved. Other helpful things you can do as a participant include:

➤ Staying focused on the meeting objectives and on the discussion

➤ Supporting useful ideas from the leader or other participants

➤ Judging the merit of ideas presented and not being distracted by delivery styles

➤ Delaying any judgment until the full idea has been presented

➤ Not allowing environmental conditions, such as noise or uncomfortable distractions, to distract you

➤ Taking well-organized notes

A good meeting participant:

➤ Prepares for the meeting

➤ Contributes ideas to the discussion

➤ Listens to the ideas of others

➤ Considers the problem objectively

➤ Contributes to the orderly conduct of the meeting

➤ Provides feedback to the meeting leader

➤ Carries out agreed-upon action

RATE YOURSELF AS A MEETING PARTICIPANT

Check (√) yes or no to each of the following questions based on how you participate in meetings.

Yes No

☐ ☐   1. Do I typically know the purpose of the meetings I attend?

☐ ☐   2. Do I have a clear understanding of my role in meetings attended?

☐ ☐   3. Do I confirm my attendance in advance of the meeting?

☐ ☐   4. Do I complete required "homework," such as looking up information or studying proposals?

☐ ☐   5. Do I arrive at meetings before they are scheduled to begin?

☐ ☐   6. Do I engage in side conversations while the meeting is in progress?

☐ ☐   7. Do I leave meetings for reasons such as non-emergency phone calls?

☐ ☐   8. Do I ask questions when I am not sure about something?

☐ ☐   9. Am I typically open to the ideas of others?

☐ ☐   10. Am I a good listener?

☐ ☐   11. Do I actively participate in discussions when I have something worthwhile to contribute?

☐ ☐   12. Do I help others stay on the subject?

☐ ☐   13. After meetings, do I take agreed-upon action?

☐ ☐   14. Do I contribute to improving meetings by giving feedback to the people who conduct them, either by a note, phone call, or visit?

☐ ☐   15. After meetings, do I inform appropriate people who did not attend about what was discussed and the outcome?

Which two or three behaviors from this list would you like to develop and practice more when you participate in meetings?

_____

_____

_____

A P P E N D I X

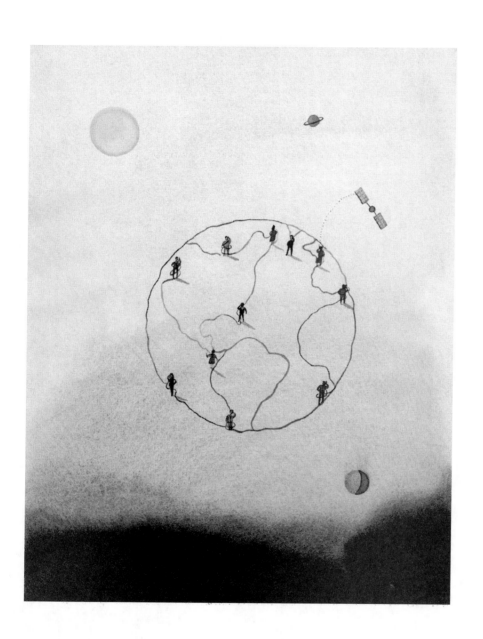

Additional Worksheets for Meeting Evaluation

Following are three additional types of worksheets you might want to use for evaluating meetings that you lead.

No further permission is needed to copy these worksheets.

MEETING EVALUATION WORKSHEET #2

1. Are agendas for meetings you attend circulated in advance or posted at the start?

   Not At All   1   2   3   4   5   Completely

2. Are you asked to provide input on the agenda?

   Not At All   1   2   3   4   5   Completely

3. Do participants monitor the way they work together?

   Not At All   1   2   3   4   5   Completely

4. Are differences among participants encouraged and explored?

   Not At All   1   2   3   4   5   Completely

5. When decisions are made, are the action steps made explicit and followed up on in writing?

   Not At All   1   2   3   4   5   Completely

6. Do participants seem aware of their use of time?

   Not At All   1   2   3   4   5   Completely

Comments:

_____

_____

_____

_____

_____

MEETING EVALUATION WORKSHEET #3

Please rate the extent to which:

	Almost Always	Never	Almost	Seldom	Sometimes	Frequently
1. Participants had a chance to express opinions.	❏	❏	❏	❏	❏	❏
2. People listened to each other.	❏	❏	❏	❏	❏	❏
3. Certain members dominated the conversation.	❏	❏	❏	❏	❏	❏
4. Some people's ideas were ignored.	❏	❏	❏	❏	❏	❏
5. People seemed satisfied with the group's decisions.	❏	❏	❏	❏	❏	❏
6. Participants seemed confused.	❏	❏	❏	❏	❏	❏
7. People seemed to understand each other.	❏	❏	❏	❏	❏	❏
8. People argued with each other.	❏	❏	❏	❏	❏	❏
9. People seemed annoyed with each other.	❏	❏	❏	❏	❏	❏

Comments:

_____

_____

_____

_____

_____

MEETING EVALUATION WORKSHEET #4

Circle the number that best describes how well our group works together.

	Low							High
Task Accomplishment	1	2	3	4	5	6	7	8
Use of Time	1	2	3	4	5	6	7	8
Use of People's Ideas	1	2	3	4	5	6	7	8
Conflict Resolution	1	2	3	4	5	6	7	8
Goal Clarity	1	2	3	4	5	6	7	8
Teamwork	1	2	3	4	5	6	7	8
Effective Listening	1	2	3	4	5	6	7	8
Leveling	1	2	3	4	5	6	7	8

What can be done to improve our working together?

_____

_____

_____

_____

_____

WORKSHEET FOR PLANNING A MEETING

This checklist can help you plan your meetings and remind you of the details you need to pay attention to as you plan.

☐ 1. **Objective:** What key results do you want to achieve?

_____

_____

☐ 2. **Timing:** How long should the meeting last? When is the best time to hold it?

_____

_____

☐ 3. **Participants:** Who should attend? Be sure to include those with authority to decide, those whose commitment is needed, and those who need to know.

_____

_____

☐ 4. **Agenda:** What items should be dealt with? Who is responsible for preparing and distributing the agenda? How will participants help in developing the agenda?

_____

_____

☐ 5. **Physical Arrangements:** What facilities and equipment are required? How should the meeting room be arranged?

_____

_____

☐ 6. **Role Assignments:** What role assignments need to be made? For example, scribe, secretary, timekeeper, and discussion moderator.

_____

_____

☐ 7. **Evaluation Method:** How will the meeting be evaluated in order to improve the next session?

_____

_____

Appendix to Part 1

Comments & Suggested Responses

Check What You Learned

1. True
2. True
3. False
4. True
5. True
6. False
7. True
8. False
9. False
10. True
11. True
12. False
13. True
14. True
15. False
16. True
17. False
18. True
19. False
20. True

Appendix to Part 2

Comments & Suggested Responses

Check What You Learned

1. True

2. True

3. True

4. True

5. False

6. False

7. False

8. True

1. Color, fonts, lettering, length of printed line, amount of information per visual are all possible answers.

2. To assure that participants in a virtual meeting all contribute, you can set up a specific protocol for how and when people speak; you can also be sure to call on everyone at least once.

Appendix to Part 3

Comments & Suggested Responses

Check What You Learned

1. Possible answers: Ensuring everyone takes part, keeping the meeting moving, limiting disruptive behavior.

2. Content, interaction, structure

3. Possible answers: Have a well-defined agenda and ground rules; keep the meeting content on topic; limit extraneous and/or repetitive questions.

4. True

5. a, c

6. Possible answers: Brainstorming to create a solution; nominal group technique to report information already known by the group.

7. False

8. True

9. True

Appendix to Part 4

Comments & Suggested Responses

Effective Use of Questions

1. c
2. h
3. f
4. d
5. i
6. e
7. g
8. h
9. a
10. b

How Would You Handle These Situations

1. 1, 2, 3, 4
2. 1, 2, 3, 4
3. 4, 3, 1, 2
4. 1, 4, 2, 3
5. 3, 4, 2, 1
6. 3, 1, 2, 4
7. 3, 2, 1, 4

Check What You Learned

1. a. Overhead questions engage the whole group and allow volunteers to respond.

   b. Direct questions focus on a selected individual to get that individual's response.

2. d

3. False

4. True

5. True

6. a, c, d

7. True

8. False

9. a. Demanding

   b. Giving in

   c. Problem solving

Appendix to Part 5

Comments & Suggested Responses

Check What You Have Learned About Evaluation & Feedback

1. False
2. True
3. False
4. True
5. False
6. True
7. True
8. False
9. False
10. True

Test Your Knowledge of Effective Meetings

1. Disagree
2. Disagree
3. Disagree
4. Agree
5. Agree
6. Agree
7. Disagree
8. Agree
9. Disagree
10. Agree
11. Agree
12. Agree
13. Agree
14. Agree
15. Agree
16. Agree
17. Agree
18. Disagree
19. Agree
20. Agree
21. Disagree
22. Disagree
23. Agree
24. Agree
25. Agree

Additional Reading

Barlow, Janelle, Peta Peter, and Lewis Barlow. *Smart Videoconferencing: New Habits for Virtual Meetings.* San Francisco: Berrett-Koehler Publishers, Inc., 2002.

Hackett, Donald and Charles Martin. *Facilitation Skills for Team Leader,* Crisp Series, 1993.

Honig, Bruce and Alain Rostain. *Creative Collaboration.* Crisp Series, 2003.

Lencioni, Patrick M. *Death by Meeting: A Leadership Fable about Solving the Most Painful Problem in Business.* San Francisco: Jossey-Bass, 2004.

Mandel, Steve. *Presentation Skills.* Crisp Series, 2000.

Raines, Claire and Linda Williamson. *Using Visual Aids.* Crisp Series, 1995.

Ramo, Simon. *Meetings, Meetings and More Meetings: Getting Things Done When People Are Involved.* Santa Monica, CA: Bonus Books, 2005.

Weatherall, Alan and Jay Nunamaker. *Getting Results from Electronic Meetings: Creative Solutions, Increased Commitment, Improved Business Processes.* London, UK: Cacklegoose Press Ltd., 2000.

Wilder, Claudyne and Jennifer Rotondo. *Point, Click and Wow!: A Guide to Brilliant Laptop Presentations.* San Francisco: Jossey-Bass, 2002.

Zelazny, Gene. *Say It with Charts: The Executive's Guide to Visual Communication.* Columbus, OH: The McGraw-Hill Companies, 2001.

Also Available

Books • Videos • CD-ROMs • Computer-Based Training Products

If you enjoyed this book, we have great news for you. There are more than 200 books available in the *Crisp Fifty-Minute™ Series*. For more information visit us online at

www.axzopress.com

Subject Areas Include:

Management

Human Resources

Communication Skills

Personal Development

Sales/Marketing

Finance

Coaching and Mentoring

Customer Service/Quality

Small Business and Entrepreneurship

Training

Life Planning

Writing